My Life After
the death of my son
… a story of miracles

KELLY KOWALL

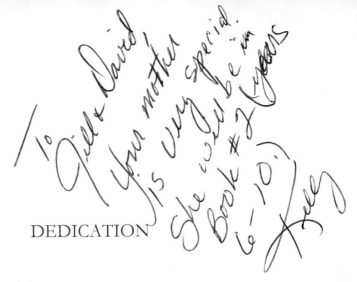

DEDICATION

I dedicate this book to:

All the people, who encouraged me to write my story.

All my friends, who read my story and gave me the confidence to publish the book.

All my friends, who helped me edit the book.

My uncle Buddy, who helped me with the re-writes and editing.

My mother, who read this book more times than I care to mention, to help me edit it.

So, if you find an editing error don't contact me, contact my friends, my uncle or my mother.

Thank you.

CONTENTS

ACKNOWLEDGMENTS

This is my personal story so there are many people named in this book, family members, friends, acquaintances and those who are no longer in my life. The views and memories expressed on these pages are mine and mine alone and do not reflect those of anyone else. Just in case, if I have written anything that someone feels is untrue or offensive, I am truly sorry for any inaccuracy. The lunacy is mine, and mine alone. My inaccuracy, my recollections and my lunacy, and you can't have them!

I hope that you enjoy reading this book and all proceeds raised will be donated to My Warrior's Place.

I do request that you do not copy any part of my book or publish it in any manner, in part or in whole, without my prior written consent. I can be reached by email at kelly@mywarriorsplace.org.

Once again, thank you for your time, and I hope you enjoy my story.

Truly yours,

Kelly Kowall - Author

My Warrior's Place

101 22nd Street NW #112

Ruskin, FL 33570

P.S. If you would like to know more about the non-profit My Warrior's Place go to

www.mywarriorsplace.org

WARRIORS PLACE
... after the Battlefield©

PRELUDE

When I was in Jr. High School, I wrote a poem about a soldier who had died on the battlefield during the Vietnam War. The poem was from the Mother's point of view. It was titled "MY SON". Little did I know that one day I would actually know how she really felt.

MY SON

My son is sleeping now,
peaceful and calm.
I watch and I listen,
while he looks at his toys;
his picture book, soldiers, and guns.
  My son is two.

My son is growing now,
talkative and alive.
I watch and I listen,
and really laugh inside;
he plays, he sings, and jokes with his friends.
  My son is five.

 My son is older now,
goes to school and strives.
I watch and I listen,
and want to help him till I die;
he studies, he's quiet, and considers
all things a challenge.
  My son is eighteen.

My son just went to war.

My son should be grown now,
married and happy.
I wish I could watch,
and I wish I could listen,
and see him again.
He would have his own

home, be talking,
and helping his children,
as I have helped him.
  My son should be thirty-two.

My son is dead.

                1938-1960
    Here lies my son who died in a war
          he didn't even start.

1 THE WEDDING

September 11th - September 19th, 2009

It was Friday, and I had just finished the last phone call for the day at work. I had already made arrangements to take the next week off. That way I could spend all my time creating the church and reception hall decorations for my stepdaughter's wedding that was to be held on Saturday the 19th. I had also committed to making a time consuming groom's cake which was to be a seven layer Czechoslovakian honey cake. It was a lot to do, but I didn't mind. I love being creative. Putting my artistic flare to use by taking something out of the ordinary and turning it into the extraordinary.

A quick dinner and then I was back in my home office constructing the frame for the twenty by twenty foot gazebo. I could envision the decorations in my mind; now I just had to bring them to reality. Later in the evening I worked on two 4 foot, two 5 foot and two 6 foot pillar floor lights for the back area of the reception hall. It was after midnight when I fell exhausted into the bed.

For the next several days I was working, from around 7:00 in the morning until after midnight, only getting a few hours of sleep. I had to get the decorations done in time. There was no way I was going to say, "I'm sorry, but I don't have your wedding decorations finished. You'll have to walk down the isle and have the reception with a few sparse ribbons and lights."

On Tuesday morning, I was working away in my home office, when Gary, my husband, opened the door. He declared that he felt I was milking the time it was taking to create the wedding decor so that I wouldn't have to take care of him. So I wouldn't have to do laundry, wouldn't have to cook him breakfast or dinner, wouldn't have to clean house.

I thought he was joking, so I replied, "Ahhh, you figured it out. As soon as you leave the house for work each day, I pop the champagne and start eating bonbons."

Gary promptly turned on his heels and slammed the door behind him as he walked out of my office and then out the front door. It was only then that I realized that he hadn't been joking. I tried to call him on his cell, but he wouldn't answer. I started to cry, not only because I was tired but because I knew that our marriage was in serious trouble.

Although I was very upset, I couldn't stop to dwell on the situation. I had to get the decorations completed. A few hours later I received an email from my husband stating that he wanted a divorce. And he wanted me out of the house by Friday.

Now I was in panic mode. My mind raced as I tried to figure out what I should do. I called my friend Anne and asked if she would let me stay at her place. She graciously agreed. But her place was too small to accommodate all the supplies I needed to create the decorations. I now knew that I was going to have to contact my stepdaughter asking for her help in finding a place where I could continue to work on the decorations. After all, it wasn't her fault that my marriage was unraveling.

I reached Lindsey at her office, apologizing for having to deliver this bad news just a few days before her wedding. I didn't know what else to do. She said that she was just getting ready to leave work for the day and would be right over, and we would figure it out together.

Once my stepdaughter arrived, she informed me that she had made arrangements to have her father stay with his mother so I would be able to stay in the house and continue working on the decorations. This week was now going to be even more stressful since not finishing the decorations was not an option.

She stayed until her father arrived home and went to confront him, to layout the current plan of action. I could hear them talking but couldn't make out what they were saying.

Finally, Lindsey came back to my office. She had learned that her dad had stopped taking his prescribed medications for a few mental disorders that were recently diagnosed. She went on to say that he didn't want to leave the house, but he had agreed to let me stay in the home until after the wedding so I could finish the decorations. Under the circumstances, this was going to be challenging, but what choice did I have?

Thursday was my birthday. I really didn't have time to celebrate. I didn't mind working on my birthday since my son Corey would not be able to call me from his FOB (Forward Operating Base) in Afghanistan. In a previous phone conversation he had let me know that his phone time was very limited and not to expect a call.

At around 8:00 p.m. the phone rang. I was pleasantly surprised to hear Corey's voice on the other end of the line.

"Happy Birthday Mom! I love you, and I miss you."

I asked him how he had gotten the phone time, and he said that one of his fellow soldiers had traded phone time with him. I was elated. We chatted for about an hour. I finally asked him if he was scared.

He said "Mom, I'm not going to lie to you. It's pretty dicey over here, and we're being shot at all the time. But if it's my time to die, I can only hope that it's over here fighting for my Country and helping to save my brothers in arms."

I confided in him what was happening on the home front, and Corey told me that he hoped I would leave Gary if things didn't get better. He then said he was going to let me go so I could get back to work.

I said, "Son, I love you, and I want you to know that I'm so proud of you. You are the best son a mother could have, and I'm so lucky that God blessed me with you."

He replied, "I love you too, Mom."

With all that I had to do, I didn't stop him from hanging up. To this day it is one of my greatest regrets.

The next day I went to the church and reception hall and began setting up all the decorations. It was a relief to know that I was able to get all of the decorations completed, but it was still a tense situation back at the house.

On Saturday, the wedding went off without a hitch. The wedding was beautiful and the bride glowed. At the reception, I was getting compliments on the decorations and the groom's cake. Many of the guests also expressed to my husband that they could not imagine the amount of time it must have taken for me to create the beautiful decor and scrumptious groom's cake.

Later in the evening my husband came over and asked me to dance; I accepted. While slow dancing, he whispered in my ear that he was sorry, that he had gotten off his medications and that he wanted to try and make the marriage work. I agreed on one condition; that he would call the psychiatrist first thing Monday morning to schedule an appointment and get back on his meds.

Late that evening, after the reception was over, we stayed to take down all the decorations and load them into the trailer. It was past 3:00 a.m. when we finally got home. I was exhausted.

2 KNOCK AT THE DOOR

Sunday, September 20th, 2009

I woke up late that Sunday. I still felt depleted of any energy. The stress of the week had taken a toll on my mind and body. I wasn't sure at this point what I was going to do. I knew our marriage was very broken, but I also knew that I was still too tired to make any rational decisions. I had been verbally and mentally abused by Gary, and I felt so beat down that I just wasn't sure I had the strength to get back up to give the marriage one more chance. After a few hours, I decided to go back to bed. I would try to make some decisions tomorrow.

At around 9:00 p.m. the phone rang. I looked at the phone. The caller ID showed that it was my ex-husband, CJ, calling. I couldn't fathom why he would be calling at this hour. I briefly thought about letting him go to voicemail, but at the last moment decided to answer it.

"Hi CJ, what's up?"

"Kelly, has the military chaplain shown up yet?"

"No, why?"

"Kelly, I don't know how to tell you this… but he is gone."

"What do you mean he is gone?!"

"Corey, he is gone."

"No… No… NO… he can't be… what happened?"

"I don't know all the details yet. I really thought that they would have arrived at your house by now. They should be there at any time."

I couldn't breathe. I couldn't think. "No... No.. I got to go now. I can't talk anymore. I have to go."

As I was hanging up the phone, my world came crashing down. This horrific news had to be a terrible joke. My son couldn't be dead. He just couldn't. I was sobbing. I needed to call his sisters, my mom and dad, my sister and brother. My mind was swirling. I sprang out of the bed and started getting dressed, pacing the floor, waiting for the knock at the door. That dreaded knock at the door.

I saw the headlights of a car pulling into the driveway through the window by the front door. I was trying to dry my eyes. He would want me to be brave, I thought. And then I heard it... the knock.

I opened the door. Standing in front of me on the porch were three men in uniform. One was a Major General, one a Chaplain and the other was the Major who would become my casualty affairs officer.

At that moment one of them pulled out a piece of paper and read, "The Secretary of the Army has asked me to express his deep regret that your son Corey died in a vehicle rollover while responding to an IED location in Viper Zabul, Afghanistan, on 20 September, 2009. The Army is conducting an investigation into the death of your son Corey.

When the investigation is complete, you will be offered the opportunity to receive a copy of the investigation. The Secretary extends his deepest sympathy to you and your Family in your tragic loss. An Army casualty assistance officer will contact you shortly. In the meantime, if you have any questions or require assistance, please contact our regional representative at 1-800-557-xxxx."

I never knew what a primal scream was until I heard it coming out of my mouth. The reality of it all was finally sinking in as I fell to my knees.

I don't remember much after that. It was as if my mind and body became frozen. I knew I was asking questions, and they were answering them, but it wasn't sinking into my brain.

3 DOVER

September 21st - September 22nd, 2009

The next morning my husband and I boarded a plane to Dover. I wanted to be there when my son's body came back to U.S. soil for the first and last time since deploying to Afghanistan. I didn't just want to be there, I had to be there. Maybe it was because I felt that if I saw his casket, I could finally accept that he had really died.

Upon arrival Gary and I were driven to the Comfort Suites Dover hotel located near the air force base. We were instructed to drop off our luggage in our room and then go to a small conference room to meet with more military personnel. We were inundated with forms that we had to sign. There were a lot of decisions that had to be made. Did we want to allow the press to be present when his coffin was transported from the plane? Did we want the autopsy results? If we chose not to receive them, we would never be able to get them.

We were informed that we would be taken to a special area to view the transfer of the flag-draped coffin from the plane to the hearse. We also were told that we would not be able to see the body or touch the casket.

I remember standing on the tarmac watching as soldiers ceremoniously carried the casket from the plane to the hearse. I remember another young woman standing beside me with an infant swaddled in a pink blanket sleeping in her arms. As she watched her husband's casket being carried from the plane to a waiting hearse, I saw her as her knees buckle. An older woman, whom I surmised was either the girls mother or mother-in-law, grabbed the baby out of the young woman's arms as she sank to the ground sobbing. I could only think that this poor baby girl would grow up never knowing her father other than from stories and pictures. Although my heart was breaking from my loss, it also broke for the wife who had just lost her husband.... for the infant who had just lost her father.... and for the mother who just lost her son. War is hell.

From Dover, I decided to fly back to Tennessee with my ex-husband CJ so that I would be able to help plan the funeral. My husband Gary flew back to Florida.

After arriving in Tennessee, Corey's father and I were told that the military would not release our son's body from Dover until we had chosen a funeral home and had a burial plot. For the next few days my life consisted of looking at cemetery plots and talking to funeral directors, fielding questions from family, friends and the press while trying to plan for the arrival of Corey's body and the funeral.

4 AIRPORT HANGER

September 24th - September 25th, 2009

My current husband had been drinking heavily on his flight into Nashville the night before my son's body was to be flown into the Smyrna, TN, airport. That evening, while in a rage, he informed me that he had decided that he did indeed want a divorce.

I told him "Now isn't the time to talk about this, and I have nothing more to say. I am tired; I am going to take my meds to help me sleep. You can talk all you want to, but I am not going to discuss this any further with you because right now I have to bury a son." I got in bed, pulled the covers up over me and cried myself to sleep.

The next morning we awoke to pouring rain. Family and friends met in the lobby of the hotel, and we boarded some vans to drive us to the Smyrna airport. Others followed us in their own vehicles. In the van Corey's father and I rode in, the silence was broken only by the sound of the pelting rain hitting the vehicle.

When we arrived at the airport, a hanger was open for us to stand in, so we didn't have to bear the elements on this solemn occasion. I couldn't believe how many people had shown up to pay their respects. There were well over 100 people standing, shaking the rain from their umbrellas and coats while we huddled in the hanger waiting for the plane to arrive.

About 10 minutes after we arrived we could hear the plane's engine getting closer before we could actually see the plane. We watched as the plane touched down on the runway and then taxied its way up in front of the hanger.

I remember feeling sorry for the CAPS (Civil Air Patrol) cadets and the soldiers in uniform whom I knew were going to have to stand out in the rain while they ceremoniously transferred Corey's flag-draped coffin from the plane to the now waiting hearse. Just as the airplane doors opened and the cadets and soldiers needed to start making their way out onto the tarmac, the rain abruptly stopped, and the sun suddenly beamed down upon us. The sky was so clear and blue. It was as if it were all orchestrated like in a movie or play.

I remember holding my breath as the coffin was lowered out of the plane and carried, by a few soldiers, to the hearse. Once the casket was slid into the hearse, we were told that the family would be allowed a few moments to gather around the casket. I felt compelled to touch the cold shiny coffin where my son now lay. Family members stepped up to touch the casket as well and then broke down as tears fell.

Then just as quickly as the rain had stopped, it started up again as if to warn us that we had used our allotted time, and we needed to leave to go back inside to the hanger. As the last person ducked under the door, we heard Kaboom! Kaboom! Kaboom! The thunder sounded like a cannon being fired.

Someone behind me said, "That sounds like a cannon being shot."

Someone else replied "Yes it does. I think that was God giving Corey a salute from heaven." They were not the only ones who felt that way.

At that time, we still didn't know if we were going to be able to have an open casket at the viewing and funeral due to Corey's injuries. Once back inside the hanger one of the funeral home directors came over to us and requested that we walk over to the hanger next door. They were going to allow us to view our son's body for the first time. His wounds had been described as being horrific, so I steeled myself for what I was going to see.

We were told that it took two morticians to work on him after he had arrived at Dover. But they had worked miracles, and other than a few spots of discoloration on his face, Corey looked like he was just sleeping. I ached to touch him, to rest my head on his chest. I had to resist the urge.

All too soon we were told it was time to go and that we would be following the hearse to the funeral home. One by one we took our seats in the van. The procession pulled out of the airport drive onto the street.

The rain was pummeling the earth once more. Looking out the windows we were awed and humbled as we saw hundreds of adults, young and old, as well as children of all ages, lined up along both sides of the roadway. For miles cars had pulled over, and the drivers and passengers stood outside of their vehicles in the pouring rain. Some stood with their hands over their hearts. Those who had served were saluting. Some were waving flags, some holding signs of condolences.

Over forty Patriot Guard Riders escorted the procession in the pouring rain with their flags proudly waving behind their motorcycles. Policemen stood at every intersection holding traffic at bay, but they stopped to salute as the hearse drove by. All these people standing along the road were soaked to the bone. That they chose to endure the massive storm and the downpour of cold driving rain paying their respects to a fallen warrior touched us deeply.

5 THE VIEWING

Saturday, September 26th 2009

The next day was the viewing at the church. My husband's oldest daughter Michelle had arrived from Georgia that morning. Her sole job was to keep her father as far away from me as possible unless we were required to sit together during any portion of the funeral events.

We arrived at the church around noon preparing ourselves for the long day ahead of us. We decided to play the music from Corey's I-Pod. It was a mixture of music from rock to bluegrass, big band to country, covering a span of decades from World War II to current. We joked that if you didn't like the song that was currently playing just wait for the next song. In a way, it really personified Corey and his many interests.

At 1:00 p.m. the first of the visitors began to file in. The line of visitors became longer and longer, snaking its way around the outside of the church and into the parking lot. I was overwhelmed by the sheer number of people who came by to pay their respects. I remember asking each person who came up to the casket how they had known my son. While many had gone to school, church or served in CAPS with him, others told me that they didn't know Corey, but they had felt compelled to come to honor him and pay their respects.

I was told later that there had been over 1800 people who came that day. Around 7:00 p.m. someone from the church came up to ask if we wanted to extend the visitation hours past 8:00 p.m. as there was still a long line of people waiting to make their way into the church. Although we agreed to extend the hours, we were able to wrap up the evening just a little after 8:00 p.m.

I was chauffeured back to the hotel and watched the weather report for the next day. The weatherman reported that there was a 60% chance for rain. I undressed and put on my pajamas, sweats and a t-shirt, and then started to write the eulogy that I would give the next day at the funeral service. The words flowed as I wrote.

"It has become immensely clear to me that words cannot adequately or sufficiently describe the meaning and value of Corey's life. To those of you here and elsewhere who had the privilege to know Corey, you already are aware of the type of person he was, and these words you will hear are already in your memory. To those who were not as fortunate, these words will give you a sense of the type of man he was.

My son was the boy who from the time he was born always had a smile on his face. He had a gentle soul. He was pure of heart and had great sensitivity for the world around him. He had a way with people that made them feel comfortable and gravitate toward him. Corey exuded kindness. He was a man of compassion.

He had a great off-beat sense of humor that could make anyone laugh, often so hard it would bring them to tears. He always let you know how much you meant to him. When he hugged you, you felt his love. He knew how to live each day to the fullest.

He respected the rules and would do the right thing even when he knew his peers would give him a hard time. Faith also always played a powerful role in Corey's decisions. Faith is why he was always incredibly optimistic. Corey would never take the easy way out. He was honest. He was loyal. He was everyone's friend. He was the perfect son.

At a very young age, Corey developed a love for his country, understood what it meant to be an American and knew he wanted to serve in the military. To do so was an honor. Military history inspired him, and if you ever walked a battlefield, toured a museum, a monument, a military base or cemetery with Corey, you appreciated being an American even more. Hero is a word often overused but in Corey's case, it is an understatement.

To everyone, I ask that you never let the mundane obligations of life distract you from what is important, the cherished gift of family and friends. Always remember to take that extra moment to kiss them or hug them, to say I love you or to let them know you care because you never know if you will ever have that opportunity again.

Lastly, I wish to express my heartfelt thanks to all those who have reached out to us throughout this most difficult time, with prayers, support, compassion and love. And to once more acknowledge how truly blessed I was to have Corey in my life.

I love you son, and will miss being with you until we

meet again in heaven.

Love always, Mom"

I was as prepared as I could be for the next day.

6 THE FUNERAL

Sunday, September 27th, 2009

The next morning I awoke to a beautiful fall day. Since the weatherman had forecasted a 60% chance of rain the night before, I felt that it was truly a miracle that the weather was absolutely perfect. I dressed and made my way down to the lobby where the family had gathered to be chauffeured to the church.

The funeral service was the epitome of Corey's personality, one moment having everyone laughing and the next bringing everyone to tears.

Corey's sisters, Kyla and Kristen, honored him by saying they were very proud that Corey was their little brother. They also acknowledged that we were honored to have sitting among us the parents of another fallen soldier, Damon Winkleman, who had also died on the 20th of September with Corey. These parents had just buried their son the day before and had driven all night to attend Corey's funeral. Their selfless act, I am sure, is a testament to the character of their son.

Kyla and Kristen then shared a poem they had written to honor both of these fine young men.

"From a toddlers age dressed in fatigues,

Corey answered the call,

that someday he would enlist,

and ultimately give his all.

He never doubted his purpose,
throughout his childhood years,
that one day he would have to rise,
far beyond his fears.

He weighed the risk,
as he counted the cost,
never thinking to become
one of those lost.

Surviving Army training,
he knew he surely could,
so on the enlistment line he signed,
to do the job he should.

Their training was meticulous,
rigorous, rugged and rough,
green young heroes were formed,
infantry men strong and decisively tough.

Forgetting the what if's, maybe's, worries,

doubts and mounting fears,

the young soldiers of Ft. Bragg,

joined operation enduring freedom,

with all their military peers.

Their duties were arduous,

requiring their courage at its best,

not a day went by,

that they were not put to the test.

Selflessly they served,

they gave and gave,

enduring hardships they fought,

for freedom they must save.

His thoughts constantly focused on love,

life and a tremendous hope,

it helped endure and encourage,

his buddies to cope.

In those final breaths,

when he breathed his last,

He had faithfully served his America,

tragically ending his life way too fast.

Each day they carried thoughts,

 of loved ones back home,

Afghanistan seemed to be,

a million miles flown.

Corey and Damon,

it was the 20th of September,

not for a moment did they think,

it would be the last day they would remember.

Corey and Damon,

your life was not in vain,

not for one of us,

will ever be the same."

They concluded the poem with Kyla stating
"Your country, and your allies salute you, Corey

Joseph Kowall and Damon Gabriele Winkleman. For greater love has no man than to lay down his life for a friend."

His girlfriend, Ashley, shared excerpts from some of their correspondences showcasing Corey's outrageous sense of humor. She stated "Recently I sent him an email listing one hundred reasons why I knew that he was the one for me. Which also included how much I missed him while he was stationed at Ft. Bragg before being deployed to Afghanistan. Due to time constraints I cannot read you all one hundred reasons so just like David Letterman, I am going to give you the top ten.

Number ten… You are always concerned about how I feel, and you go out of your way to make sure I am happy.

Number nine… Your smile is gorgeous, and I could stare at it forever.

Number eight… You call me at 4:00 in the morning just to say "I love you."

Number seven… One day without you feels like a lifetime, and I really start missing you the moment you drive away.

Number six… I love how when I think of you I see the rest of my life ahead of me, and nothing else makes sense without you there.

Number five... I love watching you play the guitar and listening to your beautiful voice when you sing to me.

Number four... I'm proud of you for becoming who you are and being proud of it no matter what anyone thinks. It makes me look up to you.

Number three... You're brave and it's sexy.

Number two... I love how you think you are lucky to be with me when I am truly the lucky one.

Number one... I love your crazy taste in music; all your outrageous dance moves, you always make me laugh, and you are pretty much hilarious.

Corey would always take the time to email me or text me back so I would like to share with you his reply. For those who know Corey personally, I apologize for not being able to read this with the same witty voice mannerisms and comic timing that Corey was known for, but this is what he said.

"Ashley, I love you, I love you, I love you, I love you, I love you, I love you, dot, dot, dot."

I know that the dot, dot, dot was his way of telling me he would love me forever. But knowing Corey he probably just got tired of writing it over and over again. Anyways, he said, "I miss you like a submarine misses the ocean's surface. I miss you like a fat kid misses cake. I miss you like an imprisoned crack addict misses freshly imported uncut Columbian bam-bam. I miss you like republicans miss Ronald Regan. I miss you like dinosaurs miss existence. I miss you like Journey misses Steve Perry. I miss you like Germany misses being a world power. I can't think of any more that are original right now, sorry. I will have to get back with you later on these similes because I have to go on guard duty."

She went on to say "His mother even once told me she was afraid that Corey would never meet a girl who could appreciate his quirkiness and truly love him for who he was. I am standing here today to reassure his mother and anyone else who may have had a similar concern that I loved Corey with all my heart."

Corey's father spoke from the heart sharing a few short stories that popped into his mind. "Standing in the kitchen one day I was doing dishes, and it was about 10 degrees outside. I was getting ready to go to bed, and I looked behind me and there was Corey walking past me with an Army issued sleeping bag. I forget what they call them, but they are kind of shaped triangular, and they zip up to where there is nothing sticking out but your face. And we had a hammock in our backyard between two oak trees, and I said, "Where are you going?"

And he said "I'm going to sleep outside tonight."

And I said "Son, that's ok with me, I'm just afraid that the department of human services is going to show up and think I made you go out there for doing something wrong."

He said, "Don't worry dad, I'll bail you out."

His fellow soldiers at Ft. Bragg would say that Corey would bring stuff home that he had found out on the field, including a door from a Huey helicopter, which I have at my house.

And they would say "what are you doing with that?"

And he would say "I found it."

And they would say "why?"

And he would reply "why not?"

He was an expert on the Vietnam war and war history in general. He truly cherished what our fallen soldiers behind him had done, and it was his calling and he knew it without a shadow of a doubt." His father went on to say "I remember the first time

Corey wanted to go to the PX because he wanted to buy some stuff and there was an old Bradley Tank parked there.'

And he said "Dad, if I can get that thing running can I take it to the house?"

And I said, "Whatever you want, son."

Some of his comrades at the base said "We kind of figured eventually one of these days he's going to drive up to the barracks in a tank" and they would say "Where did you get that?"

And he would just say, "I found it."

"Some of his comrades over there in Afghanistan said in the worst of times Corey would find something to do to make us laugh. And that is what I want everyone here to remember today. That he was here to serve not only his country, but his family, his church and his comrades. Most importantly, Corey lived his dream; he died for our country, and he is the true definition of an American hero."

7 DRIVE TO FLORIDA

September 28th - October 4th, 2009

The day after the funeral my husband, Gary, flew back home to Florida while I stayed in Tennessee for a few days with my parents, my brother and his family. The plan was to give me a few days to decompress from all the stress. Then my mother and I were going to drive my son's car back home to Florida.

Home… I realized that when I got back, I didn't really have a home.

My mind was still reeling from all that had transpired over the last two weeks. My thoughts kept turning to my son. Did he feel any pain when he was killed? What were his last thoughts before he lost consciousness? Was he happy up in heaven? Were his wounds healed? Was he talking to other warriors and veterans in heaven asking them to tell him war stories as he had when he was a child? Did he know how much we missed him?

As my mother and I started the drive back to Florida, these thoughts were still swirling around in my brain. For miles, we drove in silence. All of a sudden I realized that the questions that I had swirling around in my head were being answered on billboards by the side of the road. One read *'I'm lovin' it'* another read *'Life's Good.'* Was I going crazy? Did I really see billboards with the answers I was hoping to know? Was Corey trying to contact me to let me know that he was ok? I turned on the radio to redirect my attention.

Before long my mind wandered again, and the questions returned. The one that now dominated my mind was if Corey was really trying to contact me.

Was he really able to speak with me through these billboards? Then, just like before, another sign along the road answered me. *'CAN YOU HEAR ME NOW?'*

Was I going mad? I was afraid to ask my mother if she believed Corey could contact me from the beyond in fear that she would worry about my sanity. I didn't want to be put in a straight jacket and committed into a psycho ward.

In some ways, the answers I thought I was getting were comforting. In other ways, it was disturbing. I wanted to believe that Corey could contact me just like the stories in the bible of angels communicating with mankind, but that kind of contact in some ways seemed impossible.

What about my faith? Did I really believe the miracle stories that the bible held really happened? Stories about angels speaking to mankind, the parting of the red sea, how water was turned into wine and of Jesus walking on water. I wanted to believe, but to be honest, I wasn't sure.

While my mind whirled, I realized that I had missed the exit for the gas station miles back, and now my gas gauge was reading empty. We seemed to be in the middle of nowhere. I saw no signs for a filling station anywhere.

I prayed. And then just as I ended my prayer, I saw a sign for an exit and gas station. This station was the only building around. It had to be a mom and pop place. I pulled up to the pumps, filled up the gas tank and then went inside. Dust an eighth of an inch thick covered items on the shelves. It was dark and dingy inside.

My mind wondered again to thoughts of Corey. More questions. Then I rounded a display case and looked at a row of shelves. On the top shelf were some beautiful velvet pillows that had little sayings cross-stitched onto them. They caught my attention because they were so out of place compared to the rest of the items in the store. These pillows also had no dust on them, which was even more puzzling. But what took my breath away were the sayings.

"I am free."

"Believe."

"Heaven is beautiful"

"Have faith."

"I love you."

"God is good."

"Don't worry, be happy."

Those were the answers to the questions I had

44

had along my journey.

I didn't buy one of those pillows, and even today it is another regret that I still have. I've been tempted to drive back some day to see if I could find the station. But I don't because it would really freak me out if I were unable to find it.

We continued our travel through Georgia. Our plan was to stop around 9:00 p.m. at a quaint hotel where my mother enjoyed staying whenever she traveled to Florida. The sun was starting to set, and the streetlights were beginning to glow. Up ahead I noticed a streetlight that was burned out. Just as we drove under the light post, the light flickered to life. *Wow, that is odd*, I thought.

It took me back to a time when my children were little, and they teased me about sucking out the electric currents, as we would drive under a streetlight. I do have to admit that the number of lights that would go out as I drove under them did seem to exceed what I thought the norm would be. It was common to see three or four lights go out within a fifty-mile drive. Now instead of going out, they were coming on. Was this another way Corey was letting me know that he was indeed trying to contact me? Before we arrived at the hotel, two more lights that were out flickered to life as we drove underneath them. Now I felt certifiably insane.

8 THE HOUSE

October 4th – October 31st, 2009

Arriving at the house I had called home over the last three years, I realized that I didn't know if it would continue to be my home. I was on edge waiting for my husband to come home from work not knowing what kind of mood he would be in. I hated to throw in the towel on the marriage, but I also knew that if he wasn't going to stay on his meds, I needed to get out. Although I really didn't want to be around him right now, I had no choice. The only thing giving me comfort was knowing that as long as my mother was with me, Gary would be on his best behavior.

That evening, when Gary arrived home, he apologized for the way he had been acting, and once again told me he wanted to try to make the marriage work.

"Gary," I said, "I am willing to try but it is very important that you make sure to keep your upcoming psychiatrist appointment next week. You must let him know that you took yourself off your medications. If you didn't like the way the medications were making you feel, I am sure that the Doctor can prescribe something else."

What I didn't tell him was my decision to leave him if he didn't keep the appointment. I chose not to tell him because I didn't want it to sound like a threat. And, I wanted to see if he was really willing to continue to get help and stay on his meds. With all that had happened over the last several weeks, I just didn't have the energy to live with crazy anymore.

I informed Gary that I was going to contact a

realtor and help my mother find a house. I wanted my mom and dad to move down to Florida and live close by. I didn't tell him it would be where I would also be moving if things couldn't be worked out.

I put my suitcase away and made a phone call to a realtor I knew to get started house hunting. I also started planning a small celebration of life get together for my friends and neighbors who had known Corey that was to be held a few days later.

The next day I scheduled an appointment with a grief counselor and also joined a parents grief group called Bereaved Parents of America. As a certified life coach, I knew that getting help and some support for me was very important.

Within a few days, my mother and I had found a house we both liked. I put in an offer, and it was accepted. We would close in less than a week. The house was fully furnished, so my mother and I decided to move in immediately after we closed on the house. I told Gary I would just be gone for a few days while I helped my mother to paint and do some small renovation projects and packed only a few changes of clothes.

The next night I got an email from Gary's psychiatrist offering his condolences and giving me the names of several grief counselors. Evidently my husband had told the psychiatrist that I was in need of help dealing with my grief. He also informed me that my husband had canceled his appointment due to all that was going on with the death of my son, and when we felt up to rescheduling, to contact his office. I now knew that I needed to file for divorce. I suddenly felt relieved.

Two days later the weather turned cold. I drove to my home to retrieve some warmer clothes. When I got there, my key wouldn't unlock the front door. Gary must have changed the locks. Thank God, I remembered that the garage door was broken so I was able to get inside the house through the garage. I grabbed some more clothing and a few items that were precious to me and left. On the way back to the new house, I called a divorce attorney and asked what I should do. Then I scheduled an appointment to file for a divorce.

9 THE BOAT

November 4th – November 10th, 2009

A few days later I was driving to my appointment with my grief counselor, and in my foggy state, I turned left instead of right. I didn't drive very far before I realized my mistake. While looking for a place to turn around I drove past a boat that was up for sale. I had a fleeting thought that the boat would have been one that my son and I would have really been able to enjoy.

You see my son and I had shared a love for being out on the water. We had gotten certified as scuba divers together when he was just 13 and then re-certified when he turned 16. We loved to go fishing, kayaking, canoeing, sailing, snorkeling and scuba diving. We also really loved going out to a place called Beer Can Island in Tampa Bay looking for shark teeth.

I found a place to turn my car around and didn't think anymore about the boat. That night though, I dreamed about my son. He told me to buy the boat I had seen. He was very specific about what he wanted me to do with the boat. He insisted I provide boating trips to Veterans, Military Service Members and Families who had endured the death of a warrior. He wanted me to take them out to some of his favorite places out in Tampa Bay and on various rivers in the area. The dream woke me up, but I was happy I had had the dream. It was comforting seeing him and hearing his voice once more.

The next morning, over coffee, I told my mother about the dream. We both had a chuckle over the thought of me being a boat captain.

That night while sleeping I was awakened by the same dream. I had already been diagnosed with PTSD, and it was very important that I got a good nights sleep. Being woke up by the dream wasn't a good thing.

For the next two nights, I had the dream again. Now my PTSD symptoms (anxiety, irritability, certain noises were unbearable like nails on a chalk board while sudden noises made me jump and the constant need to be on guard) were intensifying due to lack of sleep.

On the fifth night when I was awaken by the dream, I literally sat up in bed. I looked up to heaven and said "Corey, please don't make me buy this boat, please, please, please don't make me buy this boat. You know why we always use to joke about them being called boats... **B**reak **O**ut **A**nother **T**housand!"

It took me a few hours, but I was finally able to drift back off to sleep. The next morning my mother asked if I had had the dream again.

I told her "Yes, and if I don't get a good nights sleep soon, I don't know what I'm going to do."

She suggested I call the doctor, schedule an

appointment and in the meantime, drive back to where the boat had been parked to see if it was still there. "If the boat is gone, maybe your dreams will stop," she said. "If the boat is still there, it sounds like it's going to be way out of your price range since you only have about $2500.00. Maybe knowing you can't afford it will stop the dreams."

I was willing to try anything. After calling the Dr.'s office, I jumped in my car and drove back to where I remembered the boat had been parked. The boat was still there. I pulled in for a closer look at the For Sale sign. There was no price listed, just a phone number. I pulled out my cell phone and dialed the number.

A man answered "Hello."

"Hi," I said. "I'm calling about your boat... what can you tell me about it? Does it run?"

I asked a few more questions, and then the man said "Lady, are you calling for your husband?"

"No" I answered. "I'm getting divorced."

"Well, have you ever owned a boat before?" he asked.

"No" I replied.

"Well then do you mind if I ask why you are interested in buying a boat?"

The question caught me off guard. My mind whirled. What do I say? Do I tell him the truth? He surely would think I was crazy. Think, think, think... what could I tell him that would sound reasonable? I heard myself say, "It's a little complicated. Just tell me this, how much do you want for the boat?"

"Five thousand for the boat and two thousand for the trailer it is on."

Yep, it was defiantly more than I could afford. "Thank you for your time," I said "That is way out of my price range. I'm sorry I bothered you," and I started to hang up the phone.

Just then I heard a "Lady wait, hey lady, wait."

"Yes?" I questioned.

"You never did tell me why you wanted the boat."

I sighed. Ok... I was just a phone number... I didn't think he would be able to send the people with the straight jackets after me, so I fessed up. "To tell you the truth, my son was killed in Afghanistan on September 20th and he has been coming to me in a dream. He is very insistent that I buy a boat and provide boating trips to Veterans, Military Service Members and Families who have experienced the pain of losing a warrior."

There was silence for a moment. Then I heard him say "Lady, I am a veteran, and if that is why you want to buy the boat, I will sell it to you trailer and all for $2,000.00."

Wow, that's great! I thought. Then my mind quickly began to wonder what was wrong with the boat. After all, he had just dropped the price $5,000.00. "I am interested," I said, "but would you mind if I brought a boat mechanic friend of mine by tomorrow so he can look the boat over?"

"Sure," he said. "What time would you like to meet?"

"How about 2:00 p.m.?" I asked.

"Ok, see you then" he replied.

The next day my mechanic friend Jeff and I went to look at the boat. Jeff gave it a good once over and pulled me aside "Buy the boat" he whispered to me.

"Are you sure?" I asked.

"Yes, buy the boat. I will donate my time to get it running. I think it just needs a good tune up. I will bring you receipts for plugs and a fuel filter. If after I get it running, you decide that you don't want it, I will reimburse you for the parts you have purchased plus give you $2500.00 for the boat. You have nothing to lose. You will make $500 on the deal. Just tell the guy that you will buy the boat."

We left with the boat, and two weeks later I conducted my first boating trip for a group of five Veterans. A few days later I rented a moving truck and met my soon to be ex at his home, so I could pick up my belongings and move them to my new home. There were a few things of mine that he wouldn't let me take so I took what he would let me have and left. I was just glad the divorce proceedings had been started and I could start to move on with my new life.

10 THANKSGIVING

November 24th – November 27th, 2009

I made arrangements for my friend Anne to come stay at my home and take care of my two dogs while my mother, father and I went to my brother's house in Franklin, Tennessee, for Thanksgiving. I wasn't sure I really wanted to go as I didn't feel like being with a lot of people right now. On the other hand, if I went, I would be able to visit my son's grave. My parents and I caught a direct flight to Nashville. It was great seeing my family again, but at times the large numbers of people became overwhelming, and I would retreat to my bedroom for some solitude.

I checked my email after our Thanksgiving dinner and saw that I had another email from my soon to be ex-husband. I didn't want to open it because I anticipated another ranting email where he would mentally berate me. I bit my lower lip, and I clicked on the email. My heart started to race as I read. Essentially the email said he felt that he had let me take too many items out of what was once our home, so he was going to break into my new house and take some items back.

I reached for my phone to call my girlfriend Anne who was house sitting for me. She answered on the 2nd ring. "Kelly, I am glad you called. I don't know how to tell you this, but someone has broken into your home and trashed the place. I am talking with a Hillsborough County sheriff as we speak. Here she wants to speak with you."

My heart was beating fast. I felt sick. The sheriff spoke, "Ma'am, I understand that you are going through a divorce. Is it possible that your estranged husband would have done this?"

"As a matter of fact, I know that he did it."

"How do you know that, Ma'am?" questioned the officer.

"Because he sent me an email stating that he was going to break in and take back items he felt he was entitled to."

"Was he entitled to them?"

"No. I didn't have anything of his. He was there at the house when I loaded up my stuff, so he knew what I had taken." My chest tightened. What had he stolen? What had he damaged? All I could think about was getting back home. "Ma'am, could you forward that email to me?" and she gave me her email address. "I am going to hand the phone back over to your friend; I will give you a call back if I have any more questions."

With that, Anne was back on the line. "Kelly, I am so sorry. I can't believe he did this to you after all you have been through. Don't worry. I will get things cleaned up as best I can for you. I am so mad at him... he had no right."

"I know," I said, feeling utterly defeated.

"I'll see you tomorrow" and I hung up the phone. I

forwarded the email to the officer and turned off the computer. I felt like someone had just kicked me in the gut. I was having a panic attack, I couldn't breathe. I felt sick. What more did I have to endure? I felt suicidal and didn't trust myself so I gave my mother my medications so I wouldn't be tempted to do something stupid. Once more I cried myself to sleep.

After I had arrived home, I realized that the most important item he had taken was my laptop. It had the last three years of pictures of my son on it, and I was so afraid that he would delete them. I didn't know if I could bear another loss. I felt like I was standing on a mountain top, and if just one more person did something to hit me with another blow, it would push me off the ledge that I was barely clinging to. It would be a year before I finally got my laptop. A year wondering if I had my cherished, irreplaceable pictures of my son left on its hard drive.

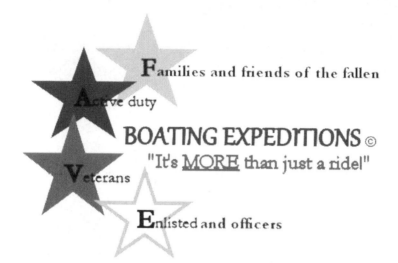

Families and friends of the fallen

Active duty

BOATING EXPEDITIONS ©

"It's MORE than just a ride!"

Veterans

Enlisted and officers

11 BECOMING A NON-PROFIT

December 2009

I continued to provide boating trips for Veterans and Families of the Fallen. It was healing for me, but it was also draining my funds. My family and friends started insisting that I find an attorney and get incorporated as a non-profit so I could start raising money to support the boating trips.

While driving to one of my appointments with

my grief counselor, I began to cry. Where was I going to find an attorney? How much would it cost? I didn't have much money so I wasn't sure I would be able to hire an attorney. Yet, if I didn't, my family and friends were going to keep hounding me. If I didn't do something soon, eventually I wouldn't be able to afford to continue the boating trips.

I began talking to my son and to God through my tears, asking them "how was I suppose to find an attorney? How was I going to pay for it?" Then I looked to my right and saw a huge sign LAW FIRM. I thought, I had a few extra minutes. I will just pull in and ask if I can speak with one of the attorneys. If they didn't practice the kind of law I needed, maybe they could refer me to one who did. Maybe they would know of one that would do it pro-bono. It doesn't hurt to ask. I pulled into the parking lot, locked my car and trotted over to the law firm.

Once inside I was greeted by the receptionist "Can I help you?"

"I don't know" I replied. "I need to speak with an attorney."

"Do you want to schedule an appointment?" she asked.

"No, I just need to ask one of your attorneys a quick question. If they can provide the services I need, then I will schedule an appointment. If they can't help me, I am hoping they can refer me to an attorney."

"Hold on." The receptionist disappeared, and a few moments later was back asking me to follow her down the hall to one of the attorney's office.

While walking she explained "He only has a few moments of time so you will need to be quick."

"That's fine," I said.

"What can I do for you?" the attorney asked as he arose from his desk and extended his hand in greeting.

Standing in his office I started explaining my plight, and of course the tears began to fall. He kindly pushed a box of Kleenexes across his desk towards me, and I gladly took one to dry my eyes and blow my nose. He then asked me to take a seat.

He said, "I am sure that you haven't noticed, but if you look around my office, you will see that I am a Veteran. I served in Desert Storm and Desert Shield."

At that point, he picked up his phone and told the receptionist to push back his next appointment. Then he turned to me and said "You're not leaving my office until we have your boating trips incorporated as a not-for-profit, and I would be honored to be one of your board members. Do you have to be anywhere?"

I told him that I had an appointment with my grief counselor, but I could call her and let her know I was going to be late. He pushed the phone my way, and I made the call.

12 CELL PHONE

Saturday, January 2nd, 2010

    Concluding a boat outing with a few veterans, we were motoring through the canals heading back to my dock when I received a call and answered my cell phone. Ending the call, I slipped the phone in my army jacket's front right breast pocket. After we docked, I started unloading the boat. I was inundated by the usual banter of:

"This was just awesome."

"It means more than you will ever know that you were so kind to me."

"This is the first time I have felt that someone truly appreciated my service. Thank you."

"Thank you for caring."

"I'm so sorry for your loss. You know your son is very proud of you."

And the one I always had to chuckle at, "I hope you realize just how much these boating trips are really needed, and I think you really could use a bigger boat."

We said our goodbyes, and I got busy cleaning the boat, getting it ready to be hoisted up on the davits. At one point, as I leaned over to attach one of the lines from the lift to one of the boat cleats, my cell phone slid out of my pocket and dropped into the water.

I stood frozen on the bow of the boat, watching in horror as my phone slowly sank into the murky depths until it was no longer visible. I thought about jumping in to try to save it, but I knew the water would be cold, I wouldn't be able to see the phone due to the visibility being less than just a few inches, and I didn't relish raking my hands through the muck trying to feel for the phone. I knew that the phone must have sunk at least four to five feet before it hit bottom, and then it would settle into a foot or more of mucky silt.

My mind raced with other options and what I could do. I decided I should just continue to put my boat up on the lift and then visit my neighborhood Verizon store to get a new phone. After all, I'd been told that my data was being backed up so I should be able to retrieve all the info that was on my now water logged phone.

When I got to Verizon, I was told that getting a new phone would not be a problem because I had insurance, BUT that the only data they backed up was my contacts and voice messages. My photos and videos were lost forever as they resided on the SIM card that was in the sunken phone. Unless I had backed them up on my computer, they were gone.

I had not backed them up and when the reality sunk in, I burst out crying. There were pictures and videos on my phone of my son going through basic training and of other visits I had had with him at Ft. Bragg before he had been deployed to Afghanistan. These were pictures and videos that could never be replaced. It felt as if I was losing my son all over again.

I know the salesman felt horrible, and I could see that he was not sure what to do with this hysterical woman who was having a total meltdown in front of him. I could tell he also felt bad. He knew that I had, just a few months ago, buried my son.

"I am so sorry," he said. "I really don't know of anyone who has ever been able to recover their phone once it went into the water. But if you can somehow retrieve it, I may be able to save the pictures and videos on the SIM card. The card can be in the water for about two hours before the images would start to deteriorate."

I left the store devastated but determined to try to rescue my phone. I had to try even though I knew the odds were against me. I jumped back into my car and drove to a friend's house who had a swimming pool. Karen would have a net, and I was definitely going to need a net if I had any hope of retrieving the phone.

With the net in hand, I made my way back to my house. I was a little apprehensive as to how much help the net was really going to be considering it had a few holes in it. But I knew no one else who had a net.

Once home, I lowered my boat back into the

water and maneuvered it to where I thought it was when my phone slipped out of my pocket. My mother was standing at the top of the dock watching.

I turned to her and said "Mom, please pray like you have never prayed before."

After saying a quick prayer myself, I dipped the net into the water until I felt it hit bottom. I then pushed it down into the silt, scooped it through the muck and then lifted the net up. I watched as about twelve inches of the brown mucky substance slowly began draining out through the netting.

After about three-quarters of the muck had leaked out, I thought I saw the corner edge of a bright blue phone case. I blinked my eyes to make sure I was seeing what I thought I saw, and there it was…. my phone. It was a miracle. With just one scoop, I had my phone. Unbelievable. I quickly swung the net around to my mother who was also standing there in shock. She grabbed the phone from the net and started to dry it off with a towel that she had brought outside in hopes that I'd get lucky.

I threw down the net and bounded up the dock stairs. Grabbing the phone from my mother's hands, I thanked her and told her I would be back as soon as I could. I jumped into my car and sped off to the Verizon store.

I ran into the store holding the phone up for the salesman to see.

"Look… can you believe it? I was able to retrieve my phone. Please tell me that you can save my pictures!"

The salesman took the phone from my hands and pulled the SIM card out. He reached for a bottle of clear solution and rinsed the SIM card and then dried it off with a cloth.

"Please tell me you are going to be able to retrieve my pictures for me" I pleaded.

"I won't know for sure until I put the SIM card into a phone. Give me your new cell phone," he said.

I handed him my phone, and he put the SIM card inside and then lifted the phone to his ear. "I can hear that it's trying to load. That is a good sign."

Then he looked at the screen. I was holding my breath and trying to read his face. I couldn't tell if he saw anything or not. Then slowly he turned the face of the phone around to me, and there I saw it. It was a picture of my son. I exhaled and once more broke down and cried as I sank to my knees thanking God for his blessings.

13 FIELD OF HONOR

Saturday, January 9th, 2010

I attended a Field of Honor ceremony that was held at the Veterans Memorial Park in Hillsborough County right off of highway 301. I had been asked to say a few words and place a flag into the ground as my son's name was to be read, along with the names of others who had died over the last few months while serving. Little did I know that three 82nd Airborne Association Members would be present.

They welcomed me with open arms and made me feel at ease.

The ceremony started with the presentation of flags by the color guard, the pledge of allegiance, the national anthem, and then the chaplain gave the benediction. After that I was introduced and gave my speech:

"First, I want to thank you for allowing me the privilege of speaking here on this special day.

As introduced, my name is Kelly and I am the proud gold star mother of SPC. Corey Kowall.

I know from talking to Gold Star Family members that sometimes a fear they may have, if their loved one, their military hero died on foreign soil, is that their loved one died without family near. Another fear that they may have is that their loved one will be forgotten.

When I hear someone express these fears, I tell them this:

The next time you talk about the loss of your loved one, with any veteran or military person who has lost a brother in arms, make sure to look into the eyes of that armed forces warrior or veteran when you are speaking. I promise you that you will see their pain... that you will realize that your fallen hero had the love of family with them when they died and you will know that they will never EVER be forgotten.

I know from talking to the soldiers who had to endure the death of my son while out on a mission.... that they feel like they failed... I try to impress upon them that unless they were GOD they didn't have the power to make those kind of life and death decisions.... and that they did not fail. They did not fail because they were there for him... they made sure that he was not alone when he took his last breath AND they made sure that he was not left alone even after he had passed away. I am truly grateful to know that he was loved and will never be forgotten. So... to all military service persons and veterans who have had to endure the death of a brother in arms.... my heart goes out to you.

As mentioned, I have founded a non-profit program.... but when given praise for what I am doing, I have to say that I can't really take the credit. I may be the person who is doing the work to make this happen along with many others who are here on this earth..... but it is really God, our veterans and our military armed forces in heaven that are leading the charge.

So I tell you this.... don't mourn our dead military heroes and veterans.... but remember them and praise them. They are still here as angels among us. Still fighting for us... still protecting us.... and still supporting their brothers-in-arms. They are still making a difference.

At this time I would like to express my sympathies to all the Gold Star Mothers, Fathers, Husbands, Wives, Siblings and Children who have endured the death of a loved one who "GAVE IT ALL" for their country. My heart aches for you.... I do know your pain.

And lastly, let me extend my condolences to anyone who has experienced the death of a veteran. Mere words can never express just how grateful I am that they were willing to wear the uniform and fight for our country so that we all can live in the land of the free. May their honor, bravery and sacrifice never be forgotten.

Thank you and God Bless!"

After I had given my speech, these three men presented me with a certificate that made Corey, a lifetime member of their association post humorously. I was so touched that they would make such a gesture and so humbled by their support.

Little did I know that one of the men would die less than eight months later, and that the other two would continue to make an impact in my life over the next five plus years.

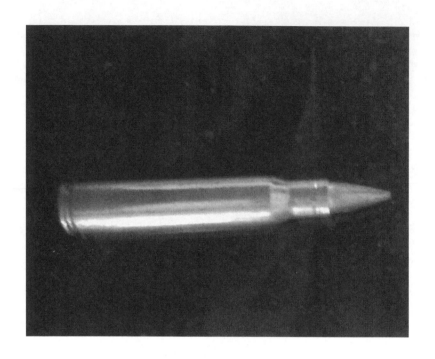

13 BULLET IN THE SAND

Wednesday, August 11th, 2010

After conducting the boating trips for 10 months, I started noticing that some of the Veterans and Active Duty Warriors I was taking on these trips still seemed to be struggling with the deaths of their brothers-in-arms. As I was healing on my own grief journey, those who were having difficulties dealing with surviving the horrors of war seemed to start standing out more and more. I kept thinking, *what is wrong with this picture?* Some of these Veterans were from the Vietnam era, so it had been 30+ years since they had lost a fellow warrior.

After one particular trip, it started to all make sense. When they are in theater, a war zone, they don't have the luxury of being able to experience the natural grief journey where ones mind shuts down and becomes frozen while the body just goes through the motions from day to day. Some of these warriors experience multiple losses over the time they are deployed along with having to witness first-hand the horrors of war.

While the military does conduct a gut wrenching ceremony to honor their fallen, that brief ceremony is all the time these warriors are really allowed to grieve. Immediately after the ceremony they have to grab their gun and helmet, and are right back out in the line of fire. They have to repress their grief for a multitude of reasons, but the most important reason is that their life and the lives on their brothers depends on them being focused and alert.

By the time they get back to U.S. soil, these

military service members have short-circuited the natural grief process for a long period of time, which makes it hard for them to get back on that grief journey. Nor do they want to. Why would they want to deal with something so painful when they just got out of hell? They don't want to hurt anymore. They just want to forget about what they had done and endured. Even if they wanted to grieve, they are not sure how to go about it because so much time has passed since the natural grief process was cut short.

The military is very good at training soldiers for war but not for grief. Grief is messy, and the military doesn't do messy.

The U.S. Department of Veterans Administration recognizes the problem of grief in soldiers returning from combat but acknowledges that little has been done to deal with it. In chapter 11 of the Department of Defense Iraq War Clinician Guide, a section entitled 'Traumatic Grief: Symptomatology and Treatment for the Iraq War Veteran' by Ilona Pivar, PhD, says that symptoms of grief are different from symptoms of PTSD and depression.

"Although research into the prevalence and intensity of grief symptoms in war veterans is limited, clinicians recognize the importance for veterans to grieve the loss of comrades," she writes.

Dr. Pivar goes on to describe that from a limited sample of Vietnam combat Veterans, "grief symptoms were detected at very high levels of intensity, thirty years post-loss." It is one of the reasons that the suicide rate is so high among our soldiers and veterans.

Once I understood the problem, I set out to find some kind of grief program that I could refer to these Veterans and Warriors when I saw one of them struggling. I performed many Internet searches using as many key words that I could think of, but I could find no program in existence. I couldn't believe that there wasn't a program out there when our country has been involved in one of the longest wars to date. Not one single program for those Warriors who have had to do many multiple tours year after year. This just couldn't be. I had to be looking in the wrong place. But as many searches as I would conduct, I couldn't find a grief program for our Veterans and Warriors.

I finally gave up searching and called one of the top grief experts in the country.

Dr. Darcie Sims answered the phone.

"Darcie Sims, how can I help you?"

"Darcie, I don't know if you will remember me, but I completed your TAPS grief and peer mentoring program at Ft. Bragg not too long ago. My name is Kelly Kowall, and I do the boating trips for Veterans, Military Service Members and Families of the Fallen down in the Tampa Bay area."

"Oh yes, I can't put your face with your name. But I do remember you because I was just so blown away that you were able to provide the boating trips so quickly after your son had died. What can I do for you?"

"Darcie, I've noticed that some of the Veterans and Military Service Members I've been taking out on my boating trips seem to be stuck in their grief over the loss of a brother-in-arms. I think it is because when they are in theater they don't have the luxury of being able to go into that frozen state that our body wants to put us in naturally. I also understand that when they get back to U.S. soil and can grieve without fear of a bullet whizzing by or the need to be on the lookout for IED's, they don't want to try and do the grief work because they would have to deal with the pain. I get that because if someone told me I had to start the grief process all over again, I would say 'no way'."

"Oh my god. It takes the mother who has lost

her son in combat to realize what is wrong with the grief process of the military." Then Darcie went on to say "No, your search results were right. Unfortunately, there is no program out there at this time to help our warriors with their grief."

"So, what are you going to do about it?" she wanted to know.

What? Did I hear her right? She wanted me to do something about this? My mind started to race, and I could only stammer "I don't know, Darcie. I need to think about it. Thank you for your time." And I hung up the phone.

The thought of trying to create a grief program that would meet the needs of those serving in the armed forces and our veterans was overwhelming. But if I didn't do something to change that void, who would? Could I live with myself if another soldier or veteran completed suicide due to the unavailability of a grief program?

I was beginning to stress out. At that moment, I started having a small meltdown at the thought of taking on such a monumental task.

To relieve the stress, I did what I usually did. I jumped on my boat and motored out to an island where my son and I use to go. I was sobbing by the time I anchored my boat.

As I started walking around the island, I began talking to God and my son. I didn't care if anyone who was out at the island could hear me or if they thought I was crazy for talking to no one that they could see. I kept asking questions to God and my son. Telling them both how hard my journey had been so far. That I didn't think I had the strength to do anything more. After all, I was already doing the boating trips. Wasn't that enough? I was just one person. The amount of money I had raised for the boating trips was peanuts compared to the amount I would need to raise to cover the cost of creating a program. And then have to raise even more money to pay for the programs. How would I ever be able to do that? I am just an ordinary person.

Finally on my third trip around the island I said, "God, if this is really what you want me to do, I will do it. But before I commit to this, I need a sign. And I am not talking about finding a pretty shell or a large sharks tooth. I am talking about a burning bush sign. If you give me a burning bush sign then, I will stop my crying and whining, and I will figure out a way to do it."

I took two more steps, and a wave washed gently over my feet and deposited a large caliber bullet there on the sand between my feet. I reached down and picked up the bullet before the next wave could take it away. The bullet was three inches in length and had the markings of L C 7 5 on the bottom of the casing. I took this bullet washing up at my feet as my burning bush sign so I dried my eyes and got back on my boat and motored back home.

After putting the boat away, I ran to the house to show my mother the bullet.

"I really think God and Corey sent me this bullet. I feel that this is a burning bush sign. What do you think?" I asked my mom.

"How else would a bullet get out to the island?" she replied.

We continued to talk about the bullet, and then we got to wondering if this bullet was safe to handle. After all, it still had to have gunpowder in it, and it had been rolling around in salt water for who knows how long.

I decided to take the bullet down to a friend who was a Vietnam Veteran. I had already taken this Veteran out on one of the boating trips, so I wasn't afraid to tell him how I had come to have this bullet. Or to ask him if he thought it was safe to handle.

"It's probably safe." he stated. "But leave it with me and I'll get the gun powder out for you. Just come back tomorrow, and I'll have it ready."

I thanked him and went back home.

The next day I returned to Jimmy's house.

"You know how you felt that this bullet washing up at your feet was a burning bush sign? Well, you don't know how much of a burning bush this bullet really is." He said.

"What do you mean?" I asked.

"Didn't you say that your son was a Vietnam history buff? he asked.

"Yes" I answered.

"Well," he continued, "this bullet was used during the Vietnam war. It's ammo for a U.S. Sniper's rifle, but this bullet is not a *current* bullet. A lot of bullets used during Vietnam are still used today, but not this one. This bullet needs to be special ordered."

Then he turned the bullet over to show me the bottom of the casing "Do you see this dimple on the bottom of this casing?" he asked, pointing out the small indentation.

"Yes" I answered.

"Well, this bullet has been fired," he said. "It's what we call a misfire. And if you know anything about guns, you know that the odds of a misfired bullet being fired are astronomical. You definitely got your burning bush."

I took the bullet and headed home in awe.

I started thinking about how I was going to create a grief and peer-mentoring program.

Sadly, Jimmy died of cancer from Agent Orange just a few years later. Warriors don't always die on the battlefield.

15 BEER CAN ISLAND

September 16ᵗʰ – September 20ᵗʰ, 2010

I knew I wanted to spend the first anniversary
of Corey's death, *his angel date*, out at one of the
favorite places my son and I like to spend time, the
Island. I asked my friend Anne if she would go with
me. It was decided that we would leave the dock

around 11:00 a.m. and have lunch on the boat.

On Thursday, a few days before the 20th, Anne flew into Tampa from Michigan. Friday, September 17th, was my birthday. My friends, Karen, Anne, Lori and I went to the Melting Pot for a wonderful fondue birthday dinner and girls night out.

On Sunday, in honor of my son, FAVE Boating Expeditions provided a boating trip for several Gold Star Family members. Later that evening, I was nervous about the upcoming day, the first anniversary of my son's angel date. Sleep eluded me for a while. When I finally drifted off, I did get a few good hours of sleep and awoke to a beautiful Florida day.

Anne and I loaded up the boat and headed out for the island. As we idled through the canals, we told Corey stories. Even the ones that we both knew so well because we were both there when the memory was made. The trip to the island was fraught with tears and laughter as we both remembered our times with Corey.

Upon arrival to the island, we anchored. We grabbed our little bags for placing our treasures in, disembarked the boat and started walking around the island in search for sharks teeth, shells, sand dollars and starfish. I had barely taken a few steps into the shallow water when I found the first shark tooth. Immediately I felt Corey's presence.

Anne and I made several trips around the island then went back to the boat to take a food break and get a drink. We marveled at how perfect the day was. How wonderful the sun felt shining down upon us. How the light breeze felt so good on our skin. I couldn't imagine a day more beautiful than the one I was having.

It wasn't long before I was ready to walk the island again. Anne decided to stay behind, so I headed back out to the shoreline by myself. On this trip around the island, I noticed a group of young men and women enjoying their time on the island. One of the young men commented on the "Army Mom" T-shirt I was wearing and inquired where my child was stationed. The young man had the tale-tell short "high and tight" haircut of a military soldier. I explained that my son had been stationed at Ft. Bragg and I was wearing a T-Shirt that I had purchased at Ft. Benning when he graduated from basic. And that he had died one year ago to the day while in Afghanistan.

The young man's name was Seth, and he had just been transferred to a local military base nearby. Seth listened as I talked about my son, and then asked if he could give me a hug.

One of the things that I missed dearly was Corey's hugs. He knew how to give a hug so that you felt hugged. I was grateful that Seth gave me a hug and couldn't help but feel that it was Corey's way of giving me a hug on this poignant date. I am still brought to tears of joy just thinking about that hug. It was truly a gift Seth gave me that will never be forgotten. It is a hug I would never have gotten if I had stayed holed up in my room waiting for the day to pass. It was a hug that I will cherish for the rest of my life.

I didn't want the day to end. I didn't want to leave the island. But as the sun began to set in the west, I knew that we needed to get back before darkness fell. Anne and I pulled up the anchors and started for home. We talked about how great the day had been. How we had felt Corey's presence, and that the only way it could have been any better was if we had been able to see the dolphins.

Just then Anne looked up into the sky and said "Yeah, Corey. Where are our dolphins?"

And then I added "Yeah, Corey. Where ARE our dolphins? We want to see dolphins!"

I had barely uttered the last sentence when Anne and I both heard it "Phff", the sound you hear when the dolphin surfaces and clears the water from his blowhole. And then we heard it again. There wasn't just one dolphin but two. They were swimming just ahead of the bow of the boat. Tears streaked down my face as Anne and I both lifted our voices to thank Corey for the dolphins. What was even more amazing was that the dolphins led the boat all the way back through the canals to the dock. Then they disappeared.

Anne commented as we unloaded the boat that she felt that one dolphin was sent for Corey, and one was sent for Damon. It was funny, but I had been thinking the same thing.

Just as we finished with putting the last few things away from the trip, we heard it again. The dolphins came back as if to say goodbye just as the sun melted into a splendid sunset.

Anne and I sat down at the table on my back porch overlooking the canal and poured our selves a shot of Jack Daniels and made a toast to Corey, thanking him for a special day. It is a day I will always remember. It was a really great day.

16 THE CROWS

September 22nd – September 28th, 2010

Two days later, I received a call from Corey's father. He informed me that his year contract with a storage unit was going to be expiring at the end of the month. His family, Corey's sisters and some of Corey's friends had already picked through Corey's belongings, and if I wanted anything, I would need to get to Tennessee before the end of the month. He went on to say that any belongings not taken by month's end would be given to Goodwill.

I grabbed a flight for Nashville on Friday, September 24th, and met with Corey's dad the next day at the storage unit to go through my son's belongings. I stored the items I had taken of my son's at my brother's house in Franklin, Tennessee. On Monday, September 27th, I jumped on another plane and flew to Ft. Wayne, Indiana, to help my Mom and Dad finish packing up their belongings to finalize their move to Florida.

On Tuesday the 28th my sister, mother and I all went to see, Jeanette Berger. She was a counselor whom we had all seen at one time or another during our lives. It was great seeing Jeannette again. We walked to her office and started talking about how Corey's death had affected all of us, and what we were doing to cope with the pain. We talked about how at times we felt that Corey was trying to contact us. About how we had seen eagles or hawks that seemed to follow us sometimes, or about certain songs that played on the radio at specific meaningful occasions or of electrical currents being affected at certain moments. We shared the fact that Corey's death had put a rift in the family. How the pain from Corey's death was intensified due to these family relationships falling apart.

All of a sudden a very huge crow showed up and started pecking on the window. The pecking became more insistent, and it started throwing itself at the window as if it were trying to break through the glass. We stopped talking and stared at the crow. Could this be an omen?

The crow flew off and we resumed our discussions. The next thing we knew it had returned but it was not alone. Now there were more crows at the window. They started squawking, pecking, and flapping their wings at the glass. They were making such a ruckus that it became impossible to carry on a conversation. People in the next office came over to see what was going on. They had never experienced anything like it. For a moment my sister and I thought it might have been Corey trying to contact us again.

But as the commotion continued we got the feeling that the crows were trying to keep us from talking. Trying to keep us from healing our broken hearts. Then someone commented that these crows felt like an evil presence. I felt chills go up and down my body. Once we acknowledged them as evil spirits they quickly flew away.

17 THE DIVORCE

Wednesday, October 8th, 2010

I walked out of the courthouse. My divorce was finalized, and I felt relieved. Now I would get my things back that my now ex-husband had taken during the break-in.

Many of the items he returned to me were not my things. They were similar to the objects that had once belonged to me, but these items looked like he had picked them up at garage sales over the last year. Sizes were wrong and brand names were not correct, some things were even broken. I could live with that.

The one item I did receive that was indeed mine was my laptop.

My heart pounded as I rushed into the house to plug it in and turn it on. Now I could check to see if my pictures were still there. My hands were shaking as I clicked on the photo program to access pictures. Then tears began to fall. Every precious picture was still there. They were all there.

"Thank you God."

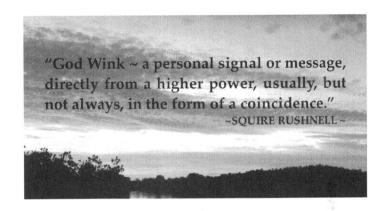

"God Wink ~ a personal signal or message, directly from a higher power, usually, but not always, in the form of a coincidence."
~SQUIRE RUSHNELL ~

18 GOD WINKS

November 8th – November 9th, 2010

On Monday, I contacted Dr. Darcie Sims at her office to tell her a story, a story about finding a bullet in the sand. When I finished telling her about my burning bush sign, she was blown away and wanted to know how she could help.

"Darcie, I need to know that you would be willing to help me create this grief and peer mentoring program. I need someone with your credentials to help me with this project." I said.

"I would love to" Darcie replied, "I think your bullet is really a God wink. But would you mind repeating your story to my husband? I feel that Tony would want to be involved."

"Sure," I said. And with that she put me on speaker phone.

I once again told my story and then asked if he wanted to help me on this endeavor. Not only was he willing to help, he wanted to be on our board of directors. I was ecstatic!

Darcie, Tony and I talked about my vision and what we would need to do to start creating this program. We also decided that it would be helpful to get together in person as soon as possible.

"Kelly, you know how busy my schedule is with my speaking engagements and workshops. It will probably be six months or more before I would have an open date." Darcie said.

Tony spoke up "Darcie, you just got in last night, and I hadn't had a chance to tell you yet, but your weekend workshop that was scheduled for the following weekend has been cancelled."

"Oh my, now that is another God wink. Wow, that is less than ten days away. What would last-minute tickets to Tampa cost?" asked Darcie.

"I don't know," said Tony, "let me check."

I could hear Tony clicking the keys on his computer as he did a search for airline tickets.

"Oh my God!" I heard him exclaim suddenly.

Oh my God what? Tickets are over $1,000.00 each? Flights are sold out? What?

"What is it T?" Darcie questioned.

"For the exact dates we can travel I can get us round-trip tickets from Seattle, WA, to Tampa, FL, for just $299.00 each. If I change the dates by just one day, the ticket price jumps up to over $1200.00." Tony answered.

"Another God wink!" declared Darcie. "That is just amazing. Book it."

With tickets purchased we discussed a game plan, and decided that we would all start taking notes of how we envisioned the program. We would compare notes in person and then chart out our plan of action. We said our goodbyes, and I hung up the phone.

That evening I received an email from a woman by the name of Cora Ruff. Cora was a professor at Howard University teaching grief to nursing students. She was a snowbird, living up north in the summer and down south in the winter.

so currently she was living in nearby Sun City Center, Florida. Cora had heard about the boating trips I was conducting and wanted to know if there was anything she could do to help. I immediately replied. I gave her my contact phone number and asked her to give me a call so we could talk.

The next day I received a call from Cora. I told her about my vision of creating a grief and peer mentoring program for our military service members and veterans who have had to cope with the death of a brother-in-arms. She thought it was a great idea but wanted to know who else was going to be involved with creating the program.

"Darcie Sims and her husband, Tony." I said.

"THE Darcie Sims?" questioned Cora.

"Well, I don't know who your THE Darcie Sims is, but mine is cofounder of Grief Inc. and the American Grief Academy and currently lives in the Seattle, Washington, area." I said.

"Oh my" uttered Cora. "I use to serve with Darcie on the board of directors for Compassionate Friends many years ago. I lost touch with her after she moved from Kentucky. If Darcie is involved, you can count me in!"

With that, we scheduled a time to meet the

next day to discuss the project and her involvement in more detail.

I emailed Darcie right after I hung up the phone and told her about my conversation with Cora. I ended the email asking for her thoughts on bringing Cora on board for this project. I got a reply back almost immediately with just two sentences written.

"I couldn't think of a better Dream Team to put this program together. I can't wait to see you both!"

I couldn't help but think I had just received another God Wink.

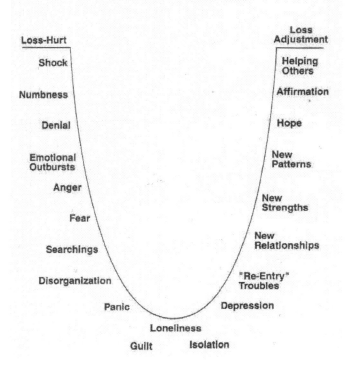

STAGES OF GRIEF

19 CREATING A PROGRAM

November 18th – November 20th, 2010

On Thursday, I met Darcie and Tony Sims at the airport. We walked downstairs to baggage claim and picked up their luggage. It was getting late and they were hungry. We decided to stop on the way to their Bed & Breakfast to get a bite to eat. Bob Evans would do the trick. We discussed our ideas over dinner, and we were very excited to get started creating a grief and peer mentoring program.

The next morning Cora joined us for breakfast, and we enjoyed getting caught up on each other's lives. After breakfast we sat outside around a large table located poolside at the Bed & Breakfast where Darcie and Tony were staying. As we were the only people on the premises at that time, we were able to work outside without interruptions.

We began with the bare bones of the program. We quickly agreed on an outline of the items that we wanted to cover during the program and the activities we wanted to conduct. After we got the bones in place, we started to put some meat on them.

We worked late into the night. We were having fun, so it didn't seem like work. The next morning we went right back at it. Later in the afternoon we started talking about what we wanted the big picture to took like and then brought everything back to present day, giving us a timeline to help us stay on track.

The next day we only had time to put in a half day of work, and then I needed to get Darcie and Tony back to the airport for their return flight home.

It was exciting working with three people who were so knowledgeable about grief. This program was going to make a positive difference in a lot of lives. It felt good knowing that I was getting to be a part of something so special and of this magnitude.

20 CANDLELIGHT CEREMONY

Sunday, December 12th, 2010

I was asked if I would be the keynote speaker at the upcoming Candlelight Ceremony for the Bereaved Parents of America event in Tampa, FL. I accepted and on Sunday, December 12th, I gave my speech.

The Journey

"You already know what I am about to say because you are alive, and a child that you love is dead. When people say they cannot imagine what it must be like to lose a child, I tell them they are right.

The only way I can even begin to convey to them the feeling of what we have been through is to tell them to imagine being in a helicopter that is traveling over an ocean. There is no land in sight. Suddenly, for no reason that YOU can comprehend, you are shoved out the door without a parachute...and then WHAM, you hit the water hard.

As the initial shock begins to wear off, you start to feel the pain, and it's excruciating. You think this can't be happening! It can't be true! But then the reality starts to seep in. You are numb with disbelief.

You don't know what to do. You feel you should do something, but you can't think. Your body moves, but your mind is not working. You look for land, but all you see is water. You know you should swim but have no clue as to which way to go.

Your body tires from treading water. It is an effort just to keep your head above the waves. It is an effort just to breathe.

You have fleeting thoughts about how it might be so much easier to just fill your lungs with water and allow yourself to sink, plummeting into the depths of the ocean below. The wind is howling, the sky is black, and the waves are enormous. You fear the storm will never end and you don't know how you will survive.

Then one day you start to realize that the turbulent storm is beginning to wane. The waves that were once over 40 feet high are subsiding. You slowly begin to realize that you are swimming even though you are unsure of your direction.

You begin thinking you may be able to survive if only you can find something to hold on to. And then you see it. It's just a plank of wood, but it allows you to grab hold, and it gives you hope.

As you drift through the water, still clinging to the board, you become aware that you are not alone. There are others in the water with you. Some have been in the water longer than you, and they have somehow managed to lash their planks together. They have built a boat, and not only have they built a boat, but they are rowing.

Throwing you a life line they pull you in. Although they greet you with open arms, they wish they did not have to welcome you aboard because they know the price you have paid for this trip is way too high.

But without hesitation they take you on board their vessel. With their knowledge and experiences through this tough journey they comfort you; they provide a safe haven for you to tell your story. They listen, and they listen, and they listen because they understand, because they get it. They encourage you to speak your child's name, to share your child's story, to share with them your journey. They give you hope. Although unsure of your destination, knowing that your life will never be the same again, you join them and slowly begin to row.

My name is Kelly Kowall, and I am the proud Gold Star mother of Specialist Corey Joseph Kowall. On September 20th, 2009, my son was killed in Afghanistan. My life as I knew it came to an end.

It was on an evening almost 15 months ago that two soldiers knocked on my door and then proceeded to push me out of that helicopter. I remember screaming during my fall, and I remember my cries of anguish and pain after hitting the water.

Although the ocean is a treacherous place when there is a storm, when the waters are calm it can be quite magical and healing. I guess that is why I envision my journey of grief to that of being adrift in an ocean as I try to survive and navigate my way to a new world.

It is also the reason that upon returning home to Florida after my son's funeral I bought a boat.

My son and I always loved spending time together on the water. So it just felt right when I began providing boat outings to a few veterans, some active duty soldiers and a couple of local Gold Star families. On these excursions, I would take them out to some of my son's favorite places. I felt it was a way that I could honor him. At the same time it was a way I could thank others for their service and sacrifice. What started out as some simple boating trips ended up being so much more than just a ride.

Soon friends started getting involved, volunteering their sailboats, fishing boats, canoes and kayaks. What we found is that these boating expeditions could be mentally and emotionally healing to everyone on board. What I found is that by reaching out and trying to do something for others during my pain, I was in fact beginning the journey to heal myself.

In April of this year, with the help of family, friends and an attorney, we founded a 501 (c) (19) non-profit organization by the name of FAVE Boating Expeditions. It is through these boating experiences that we reach out to other survivors who had experienced the loss of a military hero.

There is just something about the smell of the sea air, and feeling the sun on your face, the wind in your hair, and the gentle rocking motion of the waves. Your cares and worries just seem to drift away, and for that moment you may find peace. Although the waters are not always calm, for the moments when they are, these boating expeditions can be a vessel for hope and healing.

How do I know? Because I have been out in that ocean. I have endured many storms and I will continue to do so as they come. But mostly I know because I am a survivor.

God bless each and every one of you during this holiday season. Remember you are not alone. Remember to reach out to others. Be involved. And my hope is that each one of us will always be able to find a safe harbor when a storm blows in as we continue on our grief journey. "

This transcript of my speech was printed in the January 2011, edition of the Bereaved Parents of the USA - Tampa Area Chapter Newsletter. It was reprinted in the December 2013, edition of the Bereaved Parents of the USA – Baltimore Metropolitan Area Chapter newsletter.

21 BONE YARD BOATS

December 16th, 2010 – January 2011

One Thursday, I came across a website where people were trying to save older boats and restore them to their former glory and then find them a new home. I emailed David Irving with Bone Yard Boats.

-----Original Message----- From: Kelly Kowall Sent: Thursday, December 16, 2010 11:11 PM To: Bone Yard Boats - David Irving

Subject: I saw your website and...

David,

I was searching for a boat and came across your website. Please view our website. We are looking for a bigger boat but don't have much money as we are a newly formed non-profit. I was wondering if you could help us find a boat that would meet our needs and not need a lot of repairs. I can promise the boat would be well taken care of and have a very honorable duty taking our military heroes and families of the fallen out on boating expeditions. I have a marina in Apollo Beach, FL, that will donate a slip if we can find a boat.

Sincerely,

Kelly Kowall (Proud Gold Star Mother of Spc. Corey Kowall)

From: Bone Yard Boats - David Irving Sent: Monday, December 25, 2010 12:40 PM

To: Kelly Kowall Subject: Re: I saw your website and...

Kelly,

Thank you so much for your email, and I apologize for my delayed response. I would also like to thank you and your son, Corey, for his service and sacrifice. I feel like this is an opportunity to say something profound, but I simply cannot find the words -- other than 'thank you.'

What you are doing to support our service men & women and their families is truly wonderful, and I'd like to help out in a small way. Certainly, I will keep my eye out for an appropriate vessel for your cause. It would help if you could give me an idea of what characteristics the ideal boat would possess (i.e., power vs sail, length, etc.). By the way, what kind of boat do you use now?

What I would really like to do is to inform the Bone Yard Boats community about your efforts through a short article in the upcoming Winter 2011 issue that mails in January and on the BYB website. This would serve the dual purposes of a) possibly appealing to a member willing to donate an appropriate boat to your cause and b) spreading the word of your organization to potential donors. I can imagine a scenario in which a BYB subscriber has a boat in their yard and is having that internal struggle over whether to keep it or sell it. Knowledge of your organization gives them a third option.

I can put the story together myself based on info available on your website. However, this would be a much more compelling story if there were a personal appeal from you. So, I guess I'll present 3 options: 1) You can write it all (I may have to edit for space, etc.), 2) I can write it all, or 3) I can write up most of it and craft it in such a way that I set it up to end with a short message from you.

We'll need to work pretty quickly to get it into the Winter issue. Is this something that interests you?

If so, I would like to be very clear with my subscribers about your organization. It sounds like you have filed for non-profit status (501 C), I guess that means that donations (money &/or boat) would be tax deductible, correct? I hope to hear back from you soon, and I think that the Bone Yard Boats community would be very interested in hearing about your efforts.

Regards,

David Bone Yard Boats

From: Kelly Kowall Sent: Sat 12/25/2010 8:41 PM To: Bone Yard Boats - David Irving Subject: Re:

Re: I saw your website and...

David,

I am so touched by your response. It is Christmas Day evening and I just now had time to try and read any of my emails. As I have tears of joy running down my face right now I need to make this reply short... but the answer is yes, I do want to take you up on your offer. I will email you more answers tomorrow.

Thank you for a making this a truly wonderful Christmas. What a great present that you gave to me.

God Bless.

Sincerely,

Kelly Kowall (Proud Gold Star Mother of Spc. Corcy Kowall)

-----Original Message----- From: Kelly Kowall Sent: Sunday, December 26, 2010 05:44 PM To: "Bone Yard Boats - David Irving" Subject: reply to your questions in more detail

Dear David,

Once again, thank you so much for your email. The answers to your questions are as follows:

1.   We are currently incorporated as a non-profit in the state of Florida and have received our EIN number. We have submitted all of the paperwork required to the IRS to become a sanctioned 501 c 19 organization with the IRS.

2.   Again, you are correct on the status of donations.

3.   The boat I purchased after I returned home from my son's funeral is a 1998 Typhoon Deck Boat. It safely will hold 6 to 8 people depending on weight. I try to have a volunteer crew member for every 2 heroes we have on board so that these special guests are given undivided attention during their boating trip. Although we usually use my vessel, we have been fortunate to have a few people volunteer the use of their boat upon occasion (sailing, fishing, pontoon, kayaks, canoes, etc.).

4.   It would be great to have a large boat (motorized) that could hold at least a minimum of 15 people at one time with a galley and head. Our big dream is to one day have a large boat that would not only allow us to provide overnight expeditions and/or let us house a few heroes for a couple of days, BUT also to have some smaller boats that

would give us the opportunity to provide a variety of other boating excursions such as a sail boat and a fishing boat.

5. I have been in touch with some of FAVE Boating Expeditions' board of directors about your email. They were ecstatic and recommended that it might be good if the article was written from an "interview by you standpoint". We could even put you in contact with some of our past guest military heroes. However, we are open to whatever angle you feel might be best for your readers. The board of directors and myself also felt that it might be best if you and I could talk by phone to discuss this further due to the time constraints that you gave to make the 2011 winter newsletter. I can be reached at (813) 321-0880, but it is usually best to contact me any day between 9am and 9pm on my cell.

I look forward to hearing from you soon.

Sincerely,

Kelly Kowall (Proud Gold Star Mother of Spc. Corey Kowall)

From: Bone Yard Boats - David Irving Sent: Tuesday, December 28, 2010 10:05 AM To: Kelly Kowall Subject: Re: reply to your questions in more detail

Kelly,

Thanks for your Christmas reply and detailed follow-up email. I would love to chat with you by phone. I'm digging out from both the holiday and the substantial snowfall -- 18 inches here in our Sunday/Monday blizzard. I'll give you a call on your cell later this week. If it's not a great time for you to talk when I call, then you and I can schedule a call then.

Very much looking forward to speaking with you...

Regards,

David

Bone Yard Boats

From: Kelly Kowall Sent: Tue 12/28/2010 10:48 AM To: "Bone Yard Boats - David Irving" Subject: RE: reply to your questions in more detail

David,

Soooooooo glad to be in Florida and not buried under a foot or two of snow!!!

Good luck with your dig out and I will look forward to your call later this week.

Sincerely,

Kelly Kowall (Proud Gold Star Mother of Spc. Corey Kowall)

BONE YARD BOATS

Saving Old Boats Since 1996

Winter 2011 (Issue No. 50)

F.A.V.E. BOATING EXPEDITIONS

PROVIDES DAY OF HONOR

Shortly before Christmas, I received a brief email from Kelly Kowall asking if I could help her find a boat for her newly-formed non-profit. As you can imagine, that would not be an unusual request to receive. After all, I spend a lot of my time finding boats to present to the BYB community. Connecting boats in need of restoration with boaters looking for a project is the core of the BYB mission. However, it was the ending of Kelly's email that made this request unique: "I can promise that the boat will be well taken care of and have the very honorable duty of taking our military heroes and families of the fallen out on boating expeditions." I needed to learn more.

Kelly is the mother of Army Spc. Corey Kowall who was killed in Afghanistan on September 20, 2009, at the age of 20. Kelly told me that from the time he was 5 or 6 Corey always wanted to serve his country, and he never wavered from that desire. After returning to Florida from Corey's services in Tennessee where he grew up, Kelly spotted a "deck boat" for sale and an idea began to form. Kelly has not always been a boater, but having spent most of her life on the water she has boater friends and has always been a boat passenger. When Corey would come to visit, he would ask her to line up the boat trips. Boats and the water provided a connection between Kelly and Corey.

Kelly knew that if she went ahead and bought the boat, she'd use it to take out groups of veterans and family members who had lost a loved one. Partly, it would be her way of saying 'thank-you' for their service and their sacrifice, but, more than that, she understands that there's something magical about spending a day on the water that facilitates healing. Kelly told me, "I could feel Corey's fingertips on my back pushing me to buy the boat."

Last May, Kelly launched FAVE Boating Expeditions with a "fleet" consisting of one 1998 Typhoon Deck Boat. (F.A.V.E. = Families of the

Fallen, Active Duty, Veterans, Enlisted). Soon, others started to get involved and volunteered both themselves as crew, and sometimes their own boats and kayaks as additions to the fleet. Funded by Kelly, FAVE has had one boating trip a month since their start, and she is adamant about how these trips should go. There must be sufficient crew aboard to handle everything, not because her guests are incapable of helping out. Rather, "...this is their day of honor, and we want to wait on them."

A typical trip involves heading out into Tampa Bay from Apollo Beach and anchoring at "the island." A catered lunch is supplied. Plans may include swimming off the boat, kayaking, a walk on the beach, or perhaps some fishing. Things may be a little awkward at first. After all, these folks don't necessarily know each other, but Kelly describes seeing her passengers' bodies relaxing, their tension melting away. They start realizing that they have a lot in common. The boat becomes a safe place for them to discuss what they've been experiencing. They open up. The magic of a day on the water -- the healing -- is happening right there on the deck boat.

One former FAVE passenger reached out to me with an unsolicited email in which she talked candidly of the loss of her own son, Jacob. She also said, "Kelly rescued me." Her email ended with

"Please help support her efforts... This little lady has a tremendous heart."

Kelly also put me in touch with other past FAVE passengers, one of whom is an active duty Army staff sergeant who has served two deployments in Iraq and two deployments in Afghanistan -- so far. His FAVE experience consisted of a kayaking trip with another soldier. First, Kelly had to teach him how to kayak. He told me: "She treated you like you were her own. She made you feel like she was your mom." I took the opportunity to tell this young man that as a citizen of this country I wanted to thank him for his service. In the most respectful way imaginable, and without a second of hesitation, he responded, "I'm proud to be doing what I'm doing, sir."

My initial interactions with Kelly were about addressing the need for a bigger & better boat for her organization. The best way for me to do that is by spreading the word of her efforts to all of you. So, if there are any members of the BYB community out there with a safe craft appropriate for this purpose that you are interested in donating to this cause, please contact Kelly directly. As we talked more, however, it also became clear that boaters could also help Kelly's efforts by volunteering their own boats, time, and crew to take out veterans and

Gold Star family members wherever they may be. Kelly said, "If I have the boats and boating people, I can find the passengers." So, you don't have to be in Florida to help out, but I assure you that Kelly will insist that you adhere to her high standards in providing these folks their day of honor on the water.

For more information about FAVE and their mission, or to see some expedition photos, please check out www.favebe.com. You can also find contact details on the website.

(Story by David Irving, BYB Staff Writer)

*** *** ***

KAYAKING DOWN THE WEEKI WACHEE WITH TWO ACTIVE DUTY U.S. ARMY STAFF SERGEANTS

22 THE TEDDY BEAR

Monday, February 14ᵗʰ, 2011

I had saved several voicemail messages from

my son on my cell phone. I don't know why I never deleted them, but I was so glad that I hadn't. I loved to play them from time to time, just so I could hear his voice.

I had often thought that I would like to go to Build A Bear and create a camouflage bear. I would dress him in boots, a beret and a dog tag. I wanted to also copy the voicemail message that my son had left me on Mothers Day, 2009, and have it inserted into the bears paw.

"Hey mom, it's your son. I was just calling you to tell you Happy Mothers Day and that I love you and I miss you and I can't wait to come and see you whenever I get leave. So, um call me back I guess whenever you get this message. Um, I am on my way back to Ft. Bragg right now so I will probably be driving, so if I don't pick up the phone, then I am probably on the road. But I will call you back just as soon as I can. I love you and I miss you, and I will talk to you later. Ok bye."

Although I had been crying a lot since the death of my son, it wasn't really my personality to cry this much. And I definitely didn't like to cry in public. It was the main reason I had put off building a bear for over a year.

I had received a coupon for $20.00 off at the

local Build A Bear store and thought maybe this would be a good day to get one made. After all I had to go right by the Build A Bear store to get some printing done at a local Staples. Also, I figured, since I didn't have a guy in my life right now, it would be my valentines present to myself.

I dropped off the items I needed printed at Staples and then made my way across the street to the Brandon Mall. I parked by the entrance closest to the Build A Bear store, locked up my car and went inside.

Once in the store, I walked around to view all the options I had to build my bear. While browsing, a sales clerk came up to offer me some assistance.

"Can I help you with anything?" She asked

"Yes," I said. "I have a voice recording on my cell phone that I would like to have recorded and put inside a bear. Is there someway we can do that?"

"Usually we have you make the recording in person" she replied.

I then explained the situation and why I was hoping to be able to use the recording on my phone.

"Just a moment," she said and walked into the back room. A few moments later she returned and asked me to follow her. She introduced me to her

Manager and said that they wanted to hear the phone message so they could determine the best way to go about making the recording.

After playing the voicemail message the Manager informed me that it was too long to get it all onto one of their recording devices.

"That's ok," I said. "I would just like to get as much as we could and leave it at that."

The Manager asked the sales clerk to get one of the recorders and bring it back. Then she turned to me and said "We will record it back here so there won't be any background noise."

After the sales clerk returned, she told me to get the voicemail ready to play. She explained that she would hold the recording device up to the phone speaker as soon as I hit the play button.

I got the phone positioned so the speaker was closest to the sales clerk, and then I pushed play while she pushed the record button.

Once the message ended she said "Do you want to hear it? I'm not sure how much of the message it captured."

"No," I said, choking back tears. "It will be ok. Let's just get it put into a bear before I lose it."

The store clerk gave me a hug and then gave

me a tissue. After I dried my eyes we walked back out into the store to build my bear. About thirty minutes later I was leaving the store with my bear in hand. I walked straight to my car. Once inside the safety of my vehicle I carefully removed the bear from the box and pressed its paw.

"Hey mom, it's your son. I was just calling you to tell you HAVE A GOOD DAY and I love you and I miss you."

What? Had I heard that correctly? How could 'Happy Mothers Day' become 'Have a good day'?

I played it again; it was as clear as could be. I knew that it had been a glitch that had changed the verbiage, but for it to have manipulated the wording as it had and to end at the perfect spot was overwhelming.

I hugged the bear and cried, thanking my son and God for the perfect Valentine's Day present.

23 THE LETTER

Monday, May 30th, 2011

Throughout the spring I continued to provide boating trips as well as spending time working on the grief and peer-mentoring program.

On Memorial Day, I checked my son's Facebook page and found the following letter that had been messaged to him. The soldier who wrote it didn't know that I had access to Corey's Facebook, so I am sure that he didn't expect it to ever be read. The message made me even more determined to make sure that we would get the grief and peer-mentoring program off the ground.

'You barely knew me, but on September 20th, 2009, I was the first one to get to you. When I got to your truck, I saw D and McClelland were conscious and ran to the other side of the truck and found you. I will never forget every single sight and smell from that day. I will never forget your face. I began to work on you as you slowly slipped away. I have never been more scared in my life. I did the best I could, but I failed. I let you down. I couldn't save you. I will never forgive myself. Even when I knew you were gone, I still continued to work on you. I could not be the one to quit or give up. I stayed with you as I watched Wink slip away. I wanted to help the guys working on him, but I would not leave your side and leave you alone on that road. I moved you to the Landing Zone and stayed with you till we put you on the bird. It didn't really hit me until I had to tell your friends that you were gone. The look of utter complete sadness and grief that came over their faces along with the guilt of knowing I failed killed me. I did not just fail a fellow soldier. I failed someone's best friend. I failed someone's son. I will never forget you. You changed my life that day, and I am the man I am today because of you. A day does not go by when I don't think about that day or you. Memorial Day is just another day, but my life will be a memorial to you until the day I die. As long as I am alive there will be someone down here that remembers, honors, and still cries for you. I will never forget, and I will never forgive myself.

Love, Your brother, SGT P'

24 THE DOG TAG

Sunday, June 19th, 2011

On Fathers Day, 2011, I once again provided another boating excursion for two Gold Star Mothers, a Father, one active duty soldier and four veterans. A reporter and photographer also joined us for this expedition to write a story about the boating trips we were providing.

One of the Gold Star Mothers, Velma, told a story about how she came to possess her son's dog tag. It was a remarkable miracle story that I want to share with you.

"When Christian passed, he died on August 6th, 2009, it was because of an IED. They were coming back from a mission in a Humvee. He was with four other Marines. There was a gunner in the turret and two in the front and two in the back. As they were heading back, they ran over an IED, and there was a big explosion. They estimated that the IED weighed between 80 and 100 pounds so it was a very big explosion. Everything was pretty much destroyed."

I could see tears starting to well up in her eyes but she continued her story.

"We only got what was left of his remains, so we had to have a closed coffin at his funeral. At the funeral, I was presented with a set of dog tags, but they were not the ones Christian had been wearing that day. I asked if it was possible to get the set he had been wearing but was told that the answer was 'no' because there really wasn't anything left due the explosion being so big.

Time passed, but I couldn't shake the nagging feeling of wanting a dog tag that he had been wearing the day he was killed. Not because I didn't believe he was gone, I knew he was dead, but because I wanted to touch something that I knew he had been wearing the last day of his life.

Every day I had that thought, and I would say to God 'God you know how much I wish to have that dog tag of Christian. I wish to have it so deep in my heart, with all of my heart, and I know that you can make it happen.'

In November, three months after Christian passed, I got a message on Facebook, but I didn't check my Facebook page until months later so I didn't read this message until January, 2010.

When I opened the message, I realized how old the message was. It was from a young lady named Bonnie. It said, 'Ms. Torrez, I need to talk to you about your son Christian, please call at this number.'

I didn't recognize the phone number, but I called it that night, and she answered.

I told her 'This is Velma, Christian's mother, and I apologize for taking so long to get back with you, but I only now saw your Facebook message.'

Bonnie started talking to me saying 'Please, I am going to tell you something, but I don't want you to think I am crazy.' then she started crying and crying.

I said 'Don't worry, I won't think you are crazy. I have had a lot of unexplainable things happen since Christian's death.'

Bonnie went on to say 'I am a marine, a gunnery sergeant and a mechanic. I was working at a completely different place, at a different camp, than where Christian had died. I didn't even know Christian. But one day I was working at my camp on a Humvee that had been brought in completely destroyed. I was to try and find anything salvageable, but there was nothing. I got ready to leave the shell of the Humvee when I felt this sensation. I don't know how else to describe it but as a sensation as if someone was hugging me, keeping me in place, keeping me from leaving the Humvee.

And then I heard a voice whisper in my ear 'search'. I looked around to see who was in the area with me, but there was no one. I started to freak out and tried leaving the vehicle again, but I could not move, and I kept hearing a voice whisper in my ear over and over again 'search'.

So I started to put my hands everywhere, and then I felt something in the ruins. It was a dog tag, and I thought this was really weird. I decided to keep the dog tag because of the strange way I had come to find it. I took it back to my barracks and cleaned it up and then started a computer search of the name on the dog tag.

I learned that Christian had been killed three months earlier, and I had the feeling that I had been chosen for a special mission. To return the dog tag to his next of kin, his wife or his mother. I found out that Christian wasn't married, so I knew that the dog tag was for the mother and I started to try and find you. You see, I have three kids and I can't imagine losing one and being in your position.'

I said, 'Bonnie, you don't know how long I have been asking God for that dog tag.' That was really a special moment for me when she said that she had Christian's dog tag."

Velma went on to say, "I have spoken to Bonnie many times since that first day we talked. Bonnie tells me that every day she thinks about me, Christian and the dog tag. She knows she is a different person today because of her experience. Bonnie has said she knows God touched her that day and I know he did too."

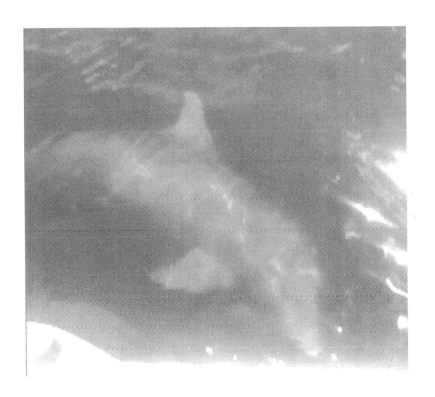

25 THE FIRST SHELL CASING

Tuesday, September 20th, 2011

On Tuesday I took my boat and headed out alone to the island. It was the 2nd anniversary of my son's angel date. I could only hope that this day would be as good as the day I spent on the island one year ago today.

As I was getting close to the island, I saw a pod of dolphins. They were splashing everywhere and having a great time. I cut the engine and just started to drift so I could go stand on the bow. A few started swimming around the boat, and I swear that one looked right at me as he rolled over on his side and swam by.

I sat on the bow and dangled my feet over the side. I was ecstatic about seeing the dolphins. They were so much fun to watch. Soon a few boats began to show up so the pod began to move out to the gulf, and then they were gone.

I started the engine, finished my trip to the island, and anchored my boat. It felt good feeling the sand between my toes as I walked around the island right at the waters edge. I was finding a lot of pretty shells and sand dollars and every once in a while I would find a shark's tooth.

On my second pass around the island, I felt the presence of my son. I could feel the weight of his hand on my shoulder as I walked. The feeling of his company was so strong, and it was so comforting. I continued about half way around the island when suddenly I could feel him leaving. I didn't want him to go, but I couldn't stop him from leaving. I had never had the urge to hug and kiss the wind as I had right then and there. As I continued to walk around, I looked down and saw a shell casing washing up on the shore. I picked it up. It was decayed, which I thought was fitting since my son was no longer alive. I also felt that it was a sign from my son letting me know that he was ok.

After having had a bullet wash up at my feet last year, a shell casing washing up didn't seem strange at all. Little did I know that that shell casing would not be the only one to be presented to me.

The rest of my day was wonderful, and I left the island to motor home under a beautiful sunset. Thank you God for another special memory.

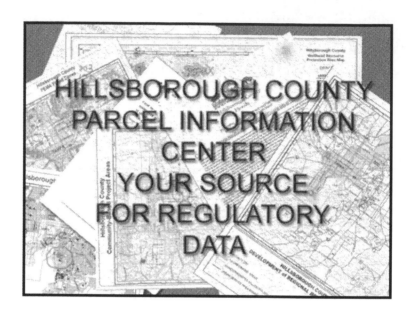

26 COMMERCIAL ZONING REQUIRED

November 2011

In November, Darcie and Tony Sims came back down to Florida to meet with Cora and me. We were starting to put the finishing touches on the grief and peer- mentoring program. While discussing the vision of how the program would work and realized that a hotel wouldn't really be the proper venue to provide the program. We needed a property that would offer a tranquil and safe setting; a place where there would not be a lot of people causing outside distractions, an area that could accommodate the activities and amenities that we wanted to provide as part of the program. In other words, a little slice of heaven.

We wondered if a Bed and Breakfast establishment might work for the venue. We knew of one that was up for sale that would be ideal. We started negotiations with the owners, but our Attorney recommended that we made sure to talk to zoning before we went any further with the plans. I scheduled a meeting with one of the zoning commissioners and had my hopes dashed as he told me that we would need a property that was zoned commercial for our endeavor.

Commercial zoning limited our possibilities and options and we knew that the price of a property, if we could find one, would soar. This property idea was starting to look like an impossibility. I was devastated. I don't know why I had let my hopes get so high. We had met a veteran who believed in what we were doing, so much so that he was willing to help us with the down payment on the Bed and Breakfast. But would he be willing to offer his financial help on another property? We had less than $500.00 in our bank account. The bank would want a much larger percentage down for a commercial piece of property, and this was probably going to crush any hopes of acquiring anything.

With all the miracles that God had worked so far to bring this program together, I just couldn't believe that he would let it fall apart over a location. I believed that there just had to be something out there, and he would reveal it to us in due time. Meanwhile, I checked for property listed on Zillow every few weeks hoping for that miracle.

27 THE SECOND SHELL CASING

Wednesday, February 1ˢᵗ, 2012

Wednesday was the 3rd Birthday of my son's that would be acknowledge without him being here on earth. I decided to spend the day out at our favorite place, Beer Can Island. I packed a picnic lunch and loaded up the boat. The day was beautiful, and I looked forward to feeling the sand beneath my feet and wading in the water as I searched for shark teeth.

On my second trip around the island, I happen to see a bullet casing lying in the water partially submerged in the sand. I found it profound that this was the third time I had received something that was part of a bullet on the third birthday I would spend without my son. I felt that this casing was my son's way of letting me know that he knew I was thinking of him on this special day and that he was happy. At least it gave me comfort to think so.

Once again, my time on the island was delightful. The weather was perfect and when it came time to depart, I really didn't want to leave. I grabbed the anchor, jumped on my boat and headed back to my dock. I loved the smell of the salt water in the air and drank in the peaceful surroundings. I reflected back over the many memories a mother has for her child; his birth, the toddler years, grade school and high school, his extra curricular activities and watching the child becoming a young man. Although I knew the pain from the loss will never go away, I realized that I had been granted a sense of peace and that this too seemed like a miracle.

I then thanked God for another wonderful day.

28 THE PROPERTY

Sunday, February 19th, 2012

On Sunday, I was working on the computer when I had this overwhelming urge to search Zillow for commercial property listings. I stopped what I was doing and entered in my search criteria onto the Zillow website. Up popped a property that was on the water in Ruskin, Florida, only 5 miles down the road from where I lived. It was a 3 bedroom / 2 bath house with a garage that had been turned into a restaurant and zoned commercial, even though it was located in a residential area. Its listing price was $250,000.00.

Hmmm, I thought. I wonder if I drove over to the property if any of the neighbors would know the owner and could give me his contact information. I decided to take a look to see if this property would work for us, and then, if it did, try my luck at finding someone in the neighborhood who could guide me to the owner.

The yard had parking in front of the house for approximately eight cars. The house was made of concrete block and looked in good shape. I thought that maybe we could build a 2nd story on the house to give us more living space. The garage area that had been added on to and turned into a commercial kitchen and restaurant would be ideal for our needs. The back yard was long and narrow, but there was potential here.

At the house next door I could hear a skill saw.

It was coming from the 2nd floor. The property had a chain link fence around it with a "Beware of Dog" sign posted prominently in plain sight. There was a set of stairs leading up to the 2nd story with a little balcony surrounding the front door. The door was wide open. When I heard the skill saw stop, I called

"YOO HOO…ANYBODY HOME?"

A man in his 60's walked out onto the balcony and looked down at me. "What do you want?" he asked.

"Do you perhaps know who happens to own this property?" I inquired, pointing to the vacant house.

"Well, as a matter of fact I own it" he stated.

"Wow," I said. "That's great! By any chance would you have a moment to talk?"

"Well, I take that back" the man said. "I did own the property, but I just sold it, and we closed on Friday."

"Oh no!" I said as I brought my hands up to the top of my head as if I just had a brain freeze.

"Why, what's wrong?" he asked.

I started to tell him my story when he stopped me.

"This sounds like this could take awhile," he said. "Why don't you come up, and I will pour us each a glass of sweet tea. I need a break anyways."

I inquired about the "Beware of Dog " sign and was told that his dog was old and would only lick you to death. With that bit of knowledge, I safely crossed into his yard and bounded up the stairs.

It was a quaint little space, long and narrow with one bedroom and bath up front and an open kitchen and living room area in the back. I seated myself on one of the barstools at the bar separating the kitchen from the living room space.

He introduced himself as Bob and proceeded to pour us each a glass of tea.

"So," he said, "tell me your story."

I introduced myself and told him about the death of my son. I told him about how I started doing boating trips and about creating the grief and peer mentoring program and how we were now looking for a special piece of property.

When I finished with my story, he reached for his computer and started typing.

"I might be able to help you" he said.

"How?" I asked.

He went on to say that he had another piece of property up the road about 1 mile. It was zoned PD-MU which was even more flexible zoning than commercial. Considering what we needed the property for, the zoning was perfect and this property was much bigger. Almost 2 acres of land and best of all, it was waterfront property.

"How much do you want for the property?" I asked.

"$580,000.00," he said.

That was over half a million dollars. There was no way we could afford that.

"I think you misunderstood," I said. "We have less than five hundred dollars in our bank account. There is just no way we could ever get a bank to loan us that kind of money."

"I could knock $100,000.00 off the price," he offered.

I said I appreciated his offer, but I didn't see how we would ever be able to come up with a down payment and find financing. Besides I thought, just 10% for a down payment would be $48,000.00, and I knew that the bank would want more than just 10% down. I was sure monthly payments would have to be well over four grand.

"Thank you for your generous offer," I said, "But there is no way we could afford something in that price range. We would be doing well to secure financing for something in the $150,000.00 to $200,000.00 range."

"Well, don't look at this as a gift," he said, "but I own the property outright so I could hold the note. What if I were to sell it to you for 4% interest over 20 years with no money down."

Had I heard him right? 4% interest and no money down?

He went on to say, "The property right now is in pretty bad shape. I've had some health problems over the last year, and the property manager let alcoholics and drug addicts move into the trailers and houses. Most have been squatting on the property for quite some time now and have pretty much destroyed the units. I just haven't had the strength emotionally, mentally, physically or financially to evict them yet. I always felt that this property was to be used for a some kind of mission, and I think God has brought you here to me."

I got goose bumps on my arms. Could this really be happening? Did I really just hear what he had said? No money down and he would hold the note at 4% interest?

"How much would that make our payments per month?" I asked.

He said, "Right around $3,000.00 per month."

Three thousand a month I thought. I hadn't even come close to raising three thousand dollars in one month during all the time I had been out working at fundraising. Two thousand had been the most I had raised in one month but usually it averaged around five hundred dollars.

"There is just no way I would be able to raise that kind of money month after month," I said. "Thank you for offering to hold the note. It was a nice of you to propose such a generous proposition, but there is just no way we could swing the payments month after month."

"Hold on," Bob said "You would be able to make the payments if you had the units rented out. In fact, if you had almost all of them rented out, you should be able to afford to pay the monthly note payment and all the utilities."

My mind got to turning, thinking of that scenario.

"Well, can we go see the property?" I heard myself ask.

Bob laughed.

"Sure, let me get my keys. If you want, you can follow me in my car as the property will be on your way back home." "

Ok," I said as I bounded down the stairs with a new burst of enthusiasm.

I followed Bob up the road to a dead end street that was on the right. We turned down that paved road and drove about 2 to 3 blocks. Bob parked his car, and I pulled up and parked behind him.

He was right about drug addicts and alcoholics squatting on the property. The place was littered with debris including tons of empty beer cans. I could see windows that were broken and everything looked filthy. The few people who were there on the property appeared drunk. Most scattered as we started to walk the property making their way into the trailers so that they wouldn't have to face Bob.

I must admit it was a little scary being there. I really didn't feel that safe, but I figured that I would be ok since I wasn't alone.

As we got down to the waters edge, I could imagine the place fixed up and beautifully landscaped. I was able to look past the disgusting stacks of old rubber tires, broken down jet skies, hulls of boats, rusted washers, dryers, refrigerators, car parts, garbage and weeds that currently littered the landscape.

"I think your offer is more than generous, but it's going to take a lot of work, time and money to get this property fixed up enough to be able to rent out the units" I said to Bob, "and I just don't see how we would be able to make the payments during the time that we were getting the property cleaned up and livable."

"Look, I really believe in what you are trying to do. What if I would hold off the first payment for a few months after we close. If you find you need extra time, we can always put a few of your first due payments on the back end of the loan." Bob replied.

I took a deep breath.

"I am very interested in your deal, but it is not solely my decision to make. I have a board of directors that I would need to run this by and get their approval." I went on to say "Bob, I really appreciate this opportunity. Thank you."

"Don't thank me" Bob replied. "Thank God."

I did just that as I drove home.

29 BOARD OF DIRECTORS

February 20th – February 27th, 2012

The next day I called a meeting of the board for that very evening. I told them about the property, and the generous offer made to purchase it. I also informed them that right now the property made Sanford & Son's Junk Yard look good, but if they could see past the mess and destruction, they would see the potential that I had seen.

We decided to meet at the property the next evening at 5:00pm. I called Bob and asked him to meet us there.

"I feel really good about this," he said, "I know that God wants me to make sure that this works out."

I thanked Bob once more for this wonderful opportunity. We said our goodbyes and I hung up the phone.

At 5:00 p.m. the next night we all met at the property. I could tell by the looks on the faces of the board members that they didn't quite see what I did and were thinking that I had to be nuts to even consider this deal.

One board member spoke up.

"Do you realize just how much money, time and supplies it will take to get this place livable? We have less than five hundred dollars currently in the bank account. I am telling you all right now, if you vote to do this; I resign."

Another board member piped up.

"Kelly, what do you have or know that makes you think you can pull this off?"

"Faith," I said. "I believe God brought us this opportunity, and I believe he will not let us fail. I can't give you any more than just my faith."

We left the property and drove back to our Attorney's office. I was asked to put together some numbers for the board to look at; what time frame did I think I could have the property fixed up and rented. When rented how much would rent generate and how much money would we need to raise to make up any deficit to cover the mortgage, utilities, insurance, etc. We decided to meet again tomorrow to talk things over and try to reach some sort of decision.

I worked well into the night crunching numbers and working up time frame scenarios. I also did some research on land prices in the area. I finally called it a night and looked forward to our meeting.

The board of directors gathered once more at the Attorney's office. I gave everyone copies of my reports and then talked about how I thought this was an opportunity we needed to act upon. There was no doubt in my mind that we should buy this property.

One of the directors spoke up.

"Kelly, you really want to do this. You really want to take a chance and try to buy this property don't you."

"Yes," I said. "I believe it is the right thing to do. That we will be glad, we took a chance. I feel that I can get the support needed from the community to make this happen."

With that, we put it to a vote. I abstained my vote. It ended up being three votes "yea" and one vote "no". The motion passed.

Immediately, the director who voted "no" stood up and said that we were being foolish and that I could expect his resignation by email this evening. With that he stormed out of the room and left the building.

I thanked the remaining directors for their support, and we called it an evening. That night I went home feeling scared but exhilarated. I also was thankful that God had given me this awesome opportunity.

30 THE PURCHASE

February 28th, 2011 - May 15th, 2012

Over the next several days, I met with Bob to discuss a game plan. In the meantime, the attorney drew up a contract to purchase the property. Bob legally made me the property manager so I could begin the eviction process for all those who were behind on their rent.

I immediately started meeting with and talking to business owners about donating supplies and services to help us with the repair work for the five mobile homes and two houses.

I also met with many civic organizations to plead for volunteers to help us with the clean up and repair work. I was truly humbled by the sheer number of people who were willing to donate or lend a hand.

It took us until May 2nd to get all but a few renters off the property. Those allowed to stay either met our military connection criteria or we were giving them time to find a new place to rent. If they paid their rent on time and followed the new guest rules, it could be beneficial for them, as well as us, while we cleaned up the property.

For the next four days, we had anywhere between 7 and 15 people out at the property hauling off the trash or making repairs on the buildings. On May 8th, many of the realtors with a local Keller-Williams office came out to the property to help paint and deep clean the units. We also had plumbers, electricians, painters, a glass company, heating and a/c companies and flooring people show up to help us turn the units into something livable.

On Tuesday, May 15th, Bob and I met at a local Title Company and closed on the property. I had to come up with a total of just $1.26 for closing costs.

I walked out thinking "what are the odds of finding a man who outright owns a perfect piece of property, who would be willing to sell it to a non-profit with no money down and delay the first mortgage payment for three months after we closed on the property."

I have to confess that my faith and endurance had been sorely tested to the point of exhaustion. It was more than just Corey that had kept me going. It was also the knowing that we were going to bring healing and hope to so many who had survived the battlefield. That we were going to be able to do more to comfort the families who were struggling with their grief. That we were going to be able to make a positive difference in the lives of those whose who have been forever changed by the tragedies of war.

All I could think about was how God sure had worked another miracle.

31 THE THIRD SHELL CASING

Saturday, May 26ᵗʰ, 2012

I had been a guest speaker at more and more events, churches and civic association venues. This day I was the keynote speaker at a Memorial Day Ceremony.

When they did the volley of rifle fire after the rendering of Taps, I thought to myself, "I wish I could have one of those shell casings." I realized that finding a shell casing after the ceremony would be impossible among all the thick grass on the cemetery grounds. Besides, trying to find the exact spot where they had shot the rifles, after the program was over, would have been just as difficult. I pushed the thought out of my mind and focused on the rest of the formal proceedings.

After the ceremony, I was talking to a few of the people who had attended the event. They were offering their condolences and telling me that my son is so proud of me. Just then another young lady walked up and quietly stood next to me as we continued to discuss how nice the ceremony had been.

Ending our conversation we all started to leave, but she stopped me. I was expecting the usual "I'm sorry for your loss", "I can't imagine" and "I want to thank you for your son's service and sacrifice." Instead she held out her hand revealing a bullet casing lying in her palm.

She said that she had found it in the grass while walking among the grave stones on her way out from the event. She had this strong feeling that she was to give me the shell casing and proceeded to ask if I would like this casing from the bullet that had been fired during the ceremony.

I took the casing from her hand and squeezed it tight in mine. I gave her a hug and thanked her for her kindness. I then silently thanked my son for sending me another bullet casing. It made a difficult day a little easier to bear.

32 TROPICAL STORM DEBBY

June 16th - June 21st, 2012

In late June, Tropical Storm Debby hit the Florida Gulf Coast. The 40+ mph winds were damaging, and the rain was relentless. As the storm intensified, I could hear shingles being ripped from the roof. The floodwaters were rising, and before long I had more than 6 inches of water on top of my enclosed patio floor.

During a lull in the storm, I went outside to survey the damage. There were large areas on the roof where the wood was now showing void of any tiles. I made a few phone calls to some veterans I knew, begging them to come over and help me tarp the roof to prevent any future damage.

My heart sank as I waded through flooded waters that were now threatening to rise high enough to invade the two houses along the water's edge. I tried to understand why God would send this storm just a few short weeks after we had closed on the property. I, along with many volunteers had just gotten the place cleaned up and now I was going to have to clean it up all over again.

I had known that the roof on the house was in bad shape when we bought the property, but I had hoped that we would have gotten at least one year out of it before it needed to be replaced. How much was a new roof going to cost, and where was I going to get the money to pay for the roof?

I tried to think about how I just needed to trust in God and let him carry my worries and heavy load.

I also really didn't have the time to fret over the damage that was already done because I had a

National BPA Convention to prepare for that week. I was to conduct one of the workshops they were providing.

It was hard not to feel defeated, and I wondered if I had made a huge mistake in buying the property. Every time the negative thoughts invaded my brain, I would stop and pray. I didn't know what else I could do under the circumstances.

Surely God had a plan. I just didn't know what it was.

33 THREE PHONE CALLS

June 22nd - June 24th, 2012

While at the National BPA convention, I received three calls that would change things for the better and once again renew and strengthen my faith.

The first call was from a woman named Sonya, whom I had met in January at a TAPS Parents

Retreat. Her son had died in Iraq several years before Corey's death. She wanted to know if we could use an RV.

"It's actually a RV Van and in great shape with only about 40,000 miles on it" she said. "I want to donate it to My Warrior's Place."

Did I hear her right? Did she want to donate an RV Van? Wow! That would really come in handy for hauling around all the items we needed to set up a booth at various events. I never could get everything required to set up a booth in my car and would always need to have someone else willing to volunteer their vehicle and time. Between the two cars we could fit all of My Warrior's Place items into them.

Sonya went on to say that they hadn't really used the RV Van since the death of her son, and it was just sitting in the driveway. I would need to fly to Pennsylvania to pick it up and drive it back, but they would really like us to have it if we thought we could use it. I told Sonya that was great, and by all means we would love to have the RV donated to us.

The second call was from a youth church pastor asking if we were in need of any help. He had heard about My Warrior's Place and his youth group was looking for a local place that they could volunteer their time and help with any cleanup that might be needed due to the storm.

The third call I received the next day. It was from a man named John who was the owner of Leprechaun Roofing in Hudson, Florida. He said that a veteran had told him about our plight and that he and his crew would like to come down in about 14 days and put on a new roof on the house over a weekend. They were going to get all the materials donated from one of his suppliers, and his crew was willing to volunteer their time and expertise to do all the work. I thanked him for all that he was about to do, and I put the dates for them to come out on my calendar.

I got to thinking. If we had just needed the roof replaced because it was in poor shape, I don't think we would have found someone to donate the roof repairs. But due to tropical storm, people were rallying around trying to help those who had been hit hard. Now I knew why God had sent the storm. He sent it so we could get a new roof and to generate more volunteers for the cleanup. The donation of the RV Van was the rainbow on top of a great weekend after the storm.

I broke down, and again tears started to flow due to this true miracle.

34 THE TAXES

Friday, July 13th, 2012

Friday, I went down to the property tax assessors office to get the paperwork that I would need to fill out and file so that the property would be tax exempt. Before we had purchased the property, we had inquired about the eligibility of the non-profit to receive the property tax exemption. We had been told that our non-profit qualified to receive the tax break, and we would not have to pay property taxes. This was crucial because, due to the zoning and location, the property taxes were very high.

Upon arriving at the office, I took a number and had a seat to wait my turn. Before long my number was called and I was greeted by a young lady who was sitting at her desk on the other side of the window.

"How may I help you?" she asked.

"I need to get the forms that will allow the property that our non-profit purchased to be tax exempt" I replied.

"Sure," she said and started typing on her computer keys and then printed out a form. "Just fill this out and attach a copy of your non-profit status and return it before February 1st."

"February 1st?" I questioned. "If I don't turn it in before the end of the year how will we get a tax exemption for the months we owned the property this year?"

"Oh," she replied, "you will not get a tax exemption for this year because you were not able to file the paperwork by February of this year. You will owe taxes for 2012, but starting in 2013 you will not owe taxes on the property."

"Why didn't someone tell me this when I called

and inquired about the tax exempt status?" I asked. "When I was told that the property would be tax exempt, I had assumed that would be from the day we closed on the property. How would I know to ask if there was any time that the property would not be considered tax exempted?"

I started to panic and felt my chest tightening. The taxes for eight months in 2012 would probably be around $10,000.00 based on what I had seen at closing just a few months before. $10,000.00! How was I going to come up with that kind of money? My mind raced, and my stomach was in knots. I felt like I was going to be sick.

"Are you ok?" the lady asked?

"I'm not sure," I said.

I took the papers she had given me and left the building.

35 KAYAK TRIP

September 19th - September 20th, 2012

I had carefully planned to spend Thursday, the third anniversary of my son's angel date, on the island. I made sure to block the date off on my calendar. On Wednesday the 19th, I rented a U-Haul trailer so that I could pick up a houseful of furniture that was being donated. Two volunteers didn't show up leaving me and one other volunteer loading the truck by our selves. Things went slower than expected, and before long we ran out of daylight with one more load to finish. We decided to come back early the next morning to finish up so I would still have time to take my boat out to the island.

The next morning all was going as planned until we returned back to the property and tried to unload the trailer. Somehow a chair had shifted while transporting the furniture. One of the legs was now caught around the bar that allows the door to roll up, keeping the door from being raised any more than about 12 inches.

I had to get the U-Haul trailer unloaded, and the trailer returned before I could go out to the island. Although I could squeeze under the door, I couldn't twist my body so I could stand up to be able to pull the chair leg free. I got a stick and tried to use it as a lever to move the chair leg, but I couldn't get enough pressure on the chair leg to get it to budge.

I watched as time slipped away. My day was starting to fall apart. I couldn't believe that this was happening, that I might not get to spend this special day out on the water and island. Moving furniture and squeezing myself into a trailer trying to wrestle with a chair is not how I envisioned this day. I was getting frustrated and angry. Why did this have to happen today of all days?

Two hours later one of the renters came home from work. He was thin and wiry. He thought he would be able to help us out, he changed clothes, then came back. After slipping under the trailer door, he managed to contort himself enough so that he could stand up in the cramped space and move the chair leg. The door rolled up, and we were then able to unload. Now I only had to return the trailer back to the U-Haul storage and rental place.

As soon as I got back from dropping off the trailer, I grabbed my things and headed to the marina where my boat was waiting for me. I walked down the ramp to the floating dock where my boat was moored. I jumped on my boat and took my seat behind the wheel. I turned the key. Nothing happened. I couldn't believe it. My battery was dead! This time tears started to fall due to frustration. It just wasn't fair.

I snatched my belongings, and on my way out, let the marina know that I needed to have the battery charged. I drove home very disappointed.

Once back at My Warrior's Place, I decided not to let what had happened keep me off the water. I grabbed a kayak and made my way down to the river. I had paddled about half way around Snake Island when the storm clouds started to roll in fast. I paddled faster heading back to the boat launch area.

Wow, this storm has come in from nowhere, I thought. Maybe all those things that happened during the day was God's way of keeping me from going out to the island. Had I gone, I would have been stranded on the island in the storm with no shelter and no way of being rescued. Just as I pulled the kayak out of the water, the first heavy drops of rain began to fall. I got the kayak put up and ran to the covered patio. Just as I ducked through the patio door another loud clap of thunder heralded a torrential downpour.

Thank God I was not stuck out in this storm because it lasted through out the rest of the evening.

36 PROJECT CORREGIDOR

November 15th - November 18th, 2012

The Sims flew into Tampa on Thursday. On Friday through Sunday, Darcie, Tony, Cora and I conducted our first Project Corregidor's Grief & Peer Mentoring Program with eight Veterans.

The first day the Veterans were very quiet, and

it was like pulling teeth trying to get them to verbally participate in the program. We had scheduled time during the program for discussion, but due to lack of participation, we ended up finishing the day's program one hour ahead of schedule.

After the Veterans had left for the evening, Tony, Darcie, Cora and I discussed the day's events. We were puzzled as to why the veterans seemed so reluctant to talk. We decided to each pull one of the veterans aside the next morning over breakfast and inquire. The next day when we asked the veterans if they had a problem with the program, we were each told pretty much the same answer.

"No, the program is awesome. We just expected that we would just be listening to lectures and taking notes. We really weren't prepared for it to be so participatory."

This day went much smoother. The veterans were participating. The energy in the room started to materialize. This day ended exactly on time.

On Sunday, we started on time, but participation was increasing. We were now having a hard time getting the veterans to stop talking. It was as if a block in a dam had been freed, and they were pouring their hearts out. We had to constantly remind them that we were running behind schedule and that if we wanted to finish the program on time, we needed for them to listen more and talk less.

It was rewarding to see the changes in the veterans in just a few short days. They now viewed things a little differently, and the healing process had taken hold.

Darcie, Tony, Cora and I went to dinner after the last Veteran left. We took the program surveys with us so we could review them and discuss our impressions of how we felt that the program had gone.

We were ecstatic to read the glowing reviews we had just received. Every Veteran had raved about the program. The only constructive criticism, repeated by every veteran, was that they wished we had made them more aware that this program would require their active participation. They also said the only thing that could make the program any better was to allow them time to meet prior to starting the first day and have them all stay in one building while going through the program.

We now knew what we had to do to tweak the program to accommodate these changes. We could see how this program was going to make a positive difference in the lives of those who had sacrificed so much for their country.

37 TAPS

March 22nd- March 25th, 2013

On Thursday, I drove up to Fort Benning, Georgia. TAPS (Tragedy Assistance Program for Survivors) was holding a weekend retreat for families of the fallen. I checked into my room at the hotel on base. It was going to be great getting to see and speak with Darcie again.

That evening TAPS held a happy hour to allow people attending the retreat to meet. I saw a young lady with a small child talking with another woman. They had to be related because there was definitely a resemblance. She looked familiar, but I couldn't place where I might have met her. Right then she saw me, and they started walking over.

When they got to me, they introduced themselves. They apologized for not knowing my name, but they had remembered seeing me at Dover standing next to them on the tarmac.

OH MY GOD! This was the wife of the soldier whose body had been transferred to Dover along with my son. This was the mother of the young lady I had seen drop to her knees in grief. Here was her daughter who was no longer an infant but a four-year-old child.

We hugged, and I told her how often I had wondered about how she was doing. How I had wondered about the little girl. How I had wondered if the mother had been able to help console her daughter from the loss of her husband the way my mother had helped to console me. I was so glad to see them.

She said that she was doing well as a single

parent and that she was going to make sure that her daughter would know her daddy through pictures and stories. The child seemed happy, but I also thought that at this age she probably really didn't comprehend missing her father since she had been fated to grow up without him. How soon would she realize what she had been forced to miss out on, that special bond between a father and a daughter. I couldn't imagine.

38 CHAPTYEAR OF 2013

March 26th- December 31st, 2012

In 2013, we continued working on My Warrior's Place transforming it into a retreat center we knew it could be. It was amazing to see so many people volunteering their time as well as organizations helping us to raise money for our property tax issue, property repairs and landscaping.

It also seemed that whenever something bad happened, something good would come out of it. I was learning not to panic at a disaster, to stay calm and have faith. Although there were not any major miracles that happened in 2013, there were a lot of little ones. Each small miracle made a huge difference and brought us that much closer to reaching our goals.

I have come to believe that God gives us many opportunities during our lifetime. We have a choice to take God up on these opportunities or to walk away. It is always our choice. I can only hope that I will always choose wisely. I hope I will have the courage it takes to take a chance when these opportunities are given to me. I hope I will live life to its fullest potential with no hesitation or regrets.

39 SPIRIT ORBS

January 30th - February 3rd, 2014

On Thursday, Darcie Sims came back to Tampa, Florida to help us further tweak the Project Corregidor Grief & Peer Mentoring Program. On the third afternoon, Darcie and I held a grief workshop for a group of veterans and gold star mothers who have endured the death of a fallen warrior. There were a few other guests who had also experienced the pain of losing someone they loved.

While we were conducting the workshop, a Sons of the American Legion group came out to My Warrior's Place to finish installing our seven flagpoles for our court of flags area.

Throughout the day, the Sons of the American Legion were texting me pictures of the progress they were making in erecting the flagpoles. I shared the pictures with those at the workshop during breaks. It was dark by the time the workshop ended. A few workshop guests had asked me to take a picture of the flagpoles once I got home and email the picture to them.

Little did anyone know that February 1st was my son's birthday. It was the fourth year I would celebrate his birthday without him here on earth.

Returning home, I grabbed my camera and rushed out to the flagpoles. Although it was dark, the light from the streetlamp illuminated the poles. They looked beautiful. I raised my camera, focused the lens and then snapped a picture. When I looked at the camera screen, I saw the picture of the flagpoles, but there were round white spots everywhere. I thought maybe the lens had dust on it, so I cleaned it with my t-shirt and took another picture. Once more I checked the camera screen to see what looked like a snowstorm around the poles. I wiped the lens again and then took one more picture. The white dots were still there. Then it hit me.

There was nothing wrong with my camera; these spheres were spirit orbs. What are orbs? Chances are, you've probably seen them before--they are the curious translucent or solid circles (usually white) that appear unexpectedly in your photos. Orbs may appear in different sizes, as a single spot or as a multitude of spots grouped together.

Some people believe that orbs are more than dust particles or drops of moisture on the lens--they are proof of guardian angels, captured on camera. When these "spirit orbs" or "angel orbs" appear near a single person or a group of people in a photo, it's a sign that they are blessed with the goodness, positive energy, and protection of angels. When orbs appear in a particular location, it's also a sign that angels are hovering nearby and the location is particularly blessed.

It was amazing. Thousands of spirit orbs were dancing around the flagpoles. It had to be the spirits of Corey and all the Veterans and Warriors in heaven down here celebrating that the flagpoles were up at My Warrior's Place on Corey's birthday. They were having a party. To make sure it was not my camera, I went inside my house and took a picture. The picture was as clear as could be. No orbs. I got goose bumps. I emailed the pictures out to those who wanted to see the flagpoles, including Darcie Sims.

The next morning Darcie and I met for breakfast and discussed the pictures. She also thought they were spirit orbs in the photos. She asked me to take some pictures again this evening after dark. This time she wanted me to take a picture of the poles, and then make a quarter turn and snap another photo. Then turn a quarter turn again so my back would now be towards the flagpoles and take another picture, and then once more turn one-quarter turn and snap another picture. She also said not to be disappointed if there were no orbs.

We then went to the manatee viewing area and leisurely enjoyed the rest of the day, retiring early so we could watch the Super Bowl.

Once the sun had set, I grabbed my camera and proceeded out to the flagpoles. I took the pictures per Darcie's instructions and reviewed them on the screen. There were a few white orbs and one orange orb in the picture I took of the flagpoles but not a single orb in the other three photos. I felt a chill, and the goose bumps returned. This truly was a special place.

40 RIP DARCIE SIMS

February 24th- February 27th, 2014

On Monday, February 24th, I received my last email from Darcie.

From: Darcie Sims – Grief Inc. Sent: Monday, February 24, 2014 3:40 PM

Kelly,

OMGosh....I cannot believe how much has

happened since I was with you at MWP. And how much time has so quickly passed....

The article is pretty good, although there are always snips and snatches of mis-information ☺ The message was clear....that MWP is a special place of hope and healing and that is what counts!

Hope the building of the fire circle went well.

I have the photo of the flagpoles in the "snow"....orb shower...on my wall in my office...as inspiration!

What's next for all of us?

Hugs and much love,

Darcie

Darcie D. Sims, Ph.D., CHT, CT, GMS Director, American Grief Academy Grief Inc.

On Thursday evening, February 27th, Darcie Sims died at home resting in her easy chair. Darcie will always be remembered for her wonderful stories, inspiring speeches and most of all her words of wisdom of which I would like to share a few here.

- We have the right to grieve; we have the privilege to grieve. Never ever forget that grief is not a sign of weakness,

nor is it a lack of faith. Grief is the price we pay for love.

- We let the pain of grief transform itself; we work our way through it, we lay down and wallow in it. You hold onto it, you wrestle with it, you have earned the right to hurt, we loved them and when they are no longer within hugs reach it hurts. So honor that, respect that, embrace that hurt and when you are through hurting…. let it go… let the hurt go.

- There are as many ways to grieve as their are people who are grieving. Please know that your own path, as long as it doesn't lead to tall buildings, sharp instruments or heavy drugs, your grief journey is the right one for you. But remember it may not be right one for the person standing next to you.

- Let go of your loss list and start making a found list.

- Don't let death negate life. They did not leave us a legacy of loss; they left us a legacy of love.

May Love be what you remember most.
~Darcie Sims

41 THE FIRE

April 23rd- May 30th, 2014

On Wednesday, I had contacted an a/c repairman to come to My Warrior's Place to look at the a/c unit that had stopped working on the yellow mobile home. He arrived and started to diagnose the problem. While working on the a/c unit, his back was to the a/c unit for the purple mobile home. All of a sudden he heard a hissing sound and then a huge explosion. As he turned to see what had exploded, he saw that the a/c unit for the purple mobile home was on fire. The flames were leaping up the side of the mobile home, and the heat was intense. He ran to shut off the electricity at the main breaker box.

It also just so happened that two guests, staying at My Warrior's Place, were walking up from the river when the explosion happened. They were right by the water faucet. They grabbed the hose and within seconds started dousing the flames with water. It was only the timing and placement of these three people at the time of the explosion and their quick thinking and actions that saved the trailer.

I shudder when I think that had this fire happened during the night or when no one was nearby, the mobile home would have burned to the ground, and our guests and their pets could have been seriously injured or killed before anyone could have responded. We also probably would have lost the shed next to the mobile home as well and possibly the yellow mobile home on the other side of the shed. If we were going to have to have a fire, the timing for this fire couldn't have been any better.

Sometimes we don't understand why bad things have to happen and we might not ever know.

It all depends on how you look at these incidents that define how you will feel about them. I like to think that we were destined to have a fire, and that God made sure that it happened when it did and that the damage was minimal and, most importantly, no one was injured or killed.

Our insurance covered the damage, and we have a better a/c unit now than we did before. God is good.

42 THE DEDICATION

Sunday, June 22nd, 2014

We had had torrential rainstorms over the two weeks leading up to our date for the dedication of the property. The ground was so water logged that the grass felt like you were walking on a giant sponge. There were large water puddles everywhere because the ground was too drenched to soak up any more water. People would ask me if I had a backup plan if the dedication date was rained out.

I would tell them,

"No. I have faith that the day will be perfect."

After all, I was constantly praying for a perfect day. I also didn't feel stressed. I wasn't worried about it. This is one time that I totally trusted God. I just knew it would be a perfect day.

I made arrangements for several tents to be delivered along with 100 chairs the day before the dedication. A few volunteers arrived to help us set everything up. The property looked beautiful. Over two years of hard work, sweat and tears had been poured into getting the retreat center landscaped and repaired.

The morning of the dedication I awoke to a perfect day. There was a gentle breeze blowing. No rain in sight. The humidity was low considering all the rain we had had, and the temperature was in the 80's.

The ceremony was spectacular and went off without a hitch.

Retired Air Force Major General David Scott was the keynote speaker. During his speech Scott said,

"It's pretty dramatic to see the changes out here, and

it's a great tribute to Kelly and a lot of volunteers. Looking back, I would not have bet my paycheck that it would be possible, but Kelly never lowered her expectations."

He was right. I never did lower my expectations. And although there were a lot of people who were very skeptical in the beginning, I thank God that there were more people that had the faith that I did.

43 CATHY'S BIRTHDAY BASH

July 23rd- August 2nd, 2014

In late July, I got a phone call from a lady named Cathy. She introduced herself, and told me that she was a cancer survivor. She went on to say that her birthday was coming up, and for the last several years she had turned her birthday party into a fundraiser for a worthy cause. She wanted to choose

My Warrior's Place to be the recipient of this year's birthday bash donations. I was so honored that she was choosing My Warrior's Place I invited her to come out to meet in person and to take a tour of the property.

Cathy and I became friends almost instantly. She is a remarkable lady, someone who also doesn't let life's blows get her down. She fell in love with the grounds of My Warrior's Place and the little cottage. She decided she wanted to stay involved with My Warrior's Place even after her party.

On Saturday, August 2nd, I drove to the VFW in Ellenton. I didn't know what to expect. I thought that maybe she would raise between $500.00 and $1,000.00 and was very excited to get there.

I was made to feel welcome from the moment I stepped foot into the Post. Cathy arrived, and we settled into having a night of fun. They sold raffle tickets and T-Shirts, and then they stopped the music so that people could give Cathy their donations in lieu of presents. People came up to the microphone and would tell how wonderful Cathy was, wish her happy birthday and then present her with a card filled with cash or a check.

The money started adding up $1000.00, $2000.00, $3,000.00. The total kept climbing

$6,000.00… $7,000.00. I was beside myself with joy and humbled by the outpouring of love and support. The total became a little over $9,800.00, so they passed the hat to get the donation up to $10,000.00. Some who had already given gave again. It was truly an amazing night.

For the first time in over a year, I was able to breathe a sigh of relief knowing that we were going to have the funds needed to pay the property taxes, due to a phenomenal little lady by the name of Cathy.

I met a few other special people that night who continue to touch my life.

I am truly blessed.

44 ANGEL DATE – FIFTH YEAR

Saturday, September 20th, 2014

September 20th, 2014, was the 5th-year anniversary of Corey's Angel date. I wrote the following on his Facebook Page:

I am Corey's mom, and I can't believe that it was five years ago today that I got the knock at the door informing me that Corey had died. Corey was not only my son, but he was my friend.

First I want to thank all of you who still post on Corey's Facebook page. I have learned —even more than I knew before—how widely and deeply Corey was loved.

Those of us who knew Corey well, know that if he were here, he would jump in right now to lighten the moment for us. Proudly sporting his military uniform, he would either quote Stewy or utter one of his wonderful Coreyisms.

One of my cherished memories of Corey is of him doing his Elvis impersonations. If you have a cherished memory of Corey, please share it with us today on the 5th anniversary of his angel date.

We miss you Corey.

I was amazed at the outpouring of stories from those who had known Corey and of pictures shared. I spent the rest of the day at two fundraisers for My Warrior's Place. It was a perfect way to honor Corey.

Although I usually spend the day out on the water, it finally hit me that it isn't so much where I honor him, but how I honor him.

Corey's death made me realize just how precious our time on earth is and to try to live each day as if it is our last. I still struggle when I have adversity in my life to stay calm and trust in God, but it is getting easier as I work hard to change my reaction habits. Consider the time you spend complaining or being negative and how your life would be different if you used that time praising or being positive.

I now try to embrace those bumps in the road knowing that something good is yet to come. I know that this new way of thinking has made a positive difference in my life, and I look forward to what the future holds for me.

EPILOGUE

September 2014 - January 2015

The rest of that autumn was fairly uneventful, but on Sunday, November the 2nd, I got a phone call about someone who wanted to downsize their boat situation. I was told that the boat owner would consider trading their boat for a smaller boat. The person calling me knew I was looking for a boat that could accommodate wheelchairs and he assured me that this boat would be ideal with some modifications. He gave me the boat owners contact information, so I quickly called the boat owner and scheduled an appointment to meet with him. On one hand I was excited that I was going to go look at their boat and discuss a possible trade. On the other hand I didn't know where I was going to get the money to have the boat modified. Still one thing I had learned over the last couple of years was not to worry. I knew that I just needed to keep moving forward in the right direction, and it would turn out ok.

On Monday, November 3rd, I got a phone call from a local foundation that wanted to schedule a time to meet with me. They were searching for a local non-profit that supported veterans and military service members. If the non-profit met their criteria, they wanted to give a grant donation. We schedule a meeting for Friday, November 11th.

On Tuesday, November 4th I met with the boat owner. I could see how his boat would be perfect for wheelchairs after a few modifications. The boat owner liked my boat and was willing to make a trade. I hated giving up the boat that my son had lead me to buy back in October of 2009, but deep down I felt that this bigger boat would be better for My Warrior's Place and our FAVE Boating Expedition program in the long run.

The next day the boat owner and I met one last time to transfer the boat titles. I then set out to find a boat mechanic and refinisher to transform the boat into a boat that could provide excursions for those even in wheelchairs.

On the 6th, I found a company who was highly recommended to refurbish boats and set off to speak with the owner in person. He was willing to donate labor for the boat project but we would need to pay for the purchase of supplies. For everything I wanted done, he estimated that the needed supplies would cost between $7,500.00 and $10,000.00. It would all depend on how much I could negotiate with companies who would be supplying the items. I told him to go ahead and get started on the re-cabling of all the wiring, tuning the engine and to start modifying the openings where you board the vessel to accommodate wheelchairs.

On Friday I met with one of the board members from the foundation and we discussed how My Warrior's Place would use the money if it were awarded to us. I told her about the boat and she informed me that the donation would be $5,000.00 if we were approved. I gave her all the information she requested and thanked her and the foundation for considering our non-profit.

On Wednesday, November 12th I got a phone call from the foundation asking if I could be at the retreat center later that day for another meeting. I told them that I had already planned on working at My Warrior's Place all day so anytime that was convenient for them was good for me.

That afternoon I was presented with a check for $10,000.00. The foundation had decided that they wanted to make sure we had the funds necessary to get the boat completely rehabbed. Their generosity brought me to tears. Immediately after their visit I was on the phone to the gentleman who was working on our boat and gave him the go ahead for making all the modification and repairs that we had discussed. Little did I know what was yet to come.... the disappointment and heartache and then the good that would come out of a very bad situation. But that is another story.

Later that November we held our Ride For The Fallen fundraiser. We also had a few fundraisers held for us by other groups and organizations. These fundraisers were to help us raise the remaining money required to pay the outstanding taxes on the property. If we failed to raise the total amount due by the deadline in February we would lose the property.

In December we had two boy scouts come and discuss doing their Eagle Scout project for My Warrior's Place. We were thrilled that they each would be able to complete one of the many projects that we needed done on the property.

Christmas brought in some more donations and then finally, on January 28th, 2015, we had the funds necessary to pay the taxes in full. As I walked out of the Hillsborough County Tax Collector's office with the paid receipt in hand, I felt compelled to take a picture of the receipt and post it on our Facebook page. It was one more obstacle that we had overcome.

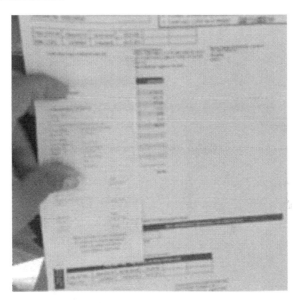

I don't know what the future holds, but one thing that I have learned and practice often is that when a tragedy occurs, take a deep breath and pray. You may not understand why the tragedy had to occur, but God does. And sometimes we learn why, and sometimes we don't.

I guess it is like when you are a child, something happens and an adult or parent expects you to do something because of what happened and you ask,

"Why?"

Sometimes you are told why. The reason is revealed and you see the bigger picture. Other times nothing is revealed and you hear the words,

"Because I said so."

At that moment we just have to accept the unknown and we just have to have a little faith.

Fate whispers to the warrior,

"You cannot withstand the storm",

and the warrior whispers back,

"I AM THE STORM."

ABOUT THE AUTHOR

Kelly Kowall is a certified grief support provider and life coach. She is also a published author, inspirational speaker and artist who resides in Apollo Beach, Florida.

59285933R00124

Made in the USA
Charleston, SC
04 August 2016